FANNING THE FLAME

FANNING THE FLAME

*Dare to Let God Kindle Your
Fire to Ignite the World*

STACY SELLS & NANCI HOGAN

YWAM Publishing
A division of Youth With A Mission
P.O. Box 55787
Seattle, Washington 98155

Dedication

A big "thank you" to Shirley Sells, Stacy's mother and our tireless editor. Thanks for the countless hours of editing, reediting, and more reediting. Your relentless red pen kept us humble, and your dedication inspired us to keep working. What will you use now as an excuse for eating Snickers bars?

We want to thank our parents, Dick and Bev Hogan and Sam and Shirley Sells. You willingly let us go on this "crazy adventure," and upheld us with daily prayer and words of encouragement. Thanks also to our churches: Church of the Apostles in Fairfax, Virginia, and Saratoga Federated Church in Saratoga, California.

We were continually encouraged and supported by friends and relatives back home. A special thanks to those who opened their homes when we returned to the States, and gave us comfortable beds and hot showers— Gayle Lemmon Fuller, Chris Williams, Theresa Tisdale, Diane Hill, Leigh Ann Hazel, and Gerry and JoAnne Fraccaro.

We could never have embarked on such a journey without the incredible hospitality of the YWAM people around the world. We recorded hundreds of stories as we listened to unselfish and unsung heroes working in a variety of conditions and locations. We only wish we could have written each person's story. However, your testimonies have left a lasting impression on our hearts, and are forever remembered by our Lord. God bless each one of you for being willing to "Go for it!"

In Memory of the Collins Family

In August, 1992, the seven members of a missionary family—father, mother, and five children—boarded a flight from Bangkok to Kathmandu. They had been on furlough in Thailand.

Their small daughter, April, had said the day before, "I want to go home." The next day, they did. Their Thai Airways flight crashed into a mountain just outside of the Nepal capital. There were no survivors.

We would like to honor the Collins family as examples of missionaries who paid the ultimate price in service to the Lord.

Table of Contents

Foreword

I saw Nanci and Stacy last month in Asia. They didn't mention anything about the adventures in this book. Instead, they were excited about the long-range effort before them. They told me about their labors on behalf of specific unreached peoples. They are tightly focused, working vigorously with a larger team, for however long it takes to see that certain select peoples are evangelized.

I was impressed with the tough resiliency of their commitment to live in an Asian city (one mentioned in their travels), working for peoples in yet other countries. It's a tough work that will take years, without question a cutting-edge endeavor of significant value. But where did they get the gumption to do it? Now I know.

As I read the book, I thought of the warning, often spoken in jest, "Do not attempt this at home."

To be sure, one could build a catalog of "Mistakes Missionaries Make" from this story. Some may consider their exploits to be exercises in squeamish naivete rather than courage. Others may ask, "What did they really accomplish?" They did get some things done, but the real story is what God was accomplishing in them for years of faith to come. And it couldn't have happened at home. And that's the value of short-term mission efforts. Leaving the shores of home, and learning at the feet of senior servants almost always lifts a life course to a new level of faith and purpose.

Look for God to move many seemingly ordinary folks to do extraordinary things. A full range of gifts and beauties of the church is being applied to complete His purposes. Nothing is more likely than the prospect of God using unlikely events to advance evangelization. In this light, the unlikely events in this book are certain to have a surprise ending in years to come.

Steve Hawthorne
The Antioch Network

A Word from Nanci and Stacy

Why would two highly educated and well-paid young women leave exciting careers in their nation's capital to embark on a journey that promised deprivation and danger? We were called upon to answer that question more than once.

Our answer lay in the hope of a reward more satisfying than any financial gain. While listening to Loren Cunningham speak one evening, we envisioned working alongside missionaries around the world, and wondered if we had what it took to become one of them.

At first, it seemed like an impossible dream. Then, unbelievably, things began to fall into place as churches, family, and friends came together to provide us with the support we needed to put our plan into action.

Once launched, we encountered tribal superstitions, threats of imprisonment, and tropical diseases. We slept in mud huts, bathed from buckets of icy water, and ate things we dared not identify. We talked our way into and out of more than a few countries. Whenever we thought we had things under control, a new surprise would loom up to test and taunt us.

We watched ordinary people transcend extraordinary circumstances, and witnessed the love of Christ translated into countless languages and acts. We saw our own faith grow in depth along the way.

Would we do it again? You bet we would!

In writing this book, we hope to put some myths to rest, to encourage the reader to dream bigger dreams, and to offer the assurance that all things are possible through Christ.

Come share our adventure.

1

Is That Really You, God? (Nanci)

I was fearless right up to the minute I stepped on the plane. Well, almost. Actually, a tiny shred of fear began to creep in at our going-away party.

Stacy was standing at a huge world map, pointing out places with exotic names. She was beaming, loving every question and look of awe.

What a ham! I thought. That was when I got this crazy, queasy feeling in the pit of my stomach. Okay, maybe it was fear. Anyway, I remember wondering how I ever got myself into this.

It began a year earlier when I attended a Youth With A Mission meeting in Washington, D.C. with my roommate, Stacy Sells. YWAM is a large, interconfessional missions organization with members stationed around the world. Its founder, Loren Cunningham, was speaking that evening.

During the question and answer period, a man rose. "Loren," he asked, "your stories about how God uses people of all ages and abilities are so inspiring. Why haven't we heard more of them?"

"We're too busy 'doing it' to write about it," Loren said. "Do you know how we can spread the word?"

My heart leapt.

Driving home, Stacy said what I had been thinking. We were healthy, in our mid-20s, and unattached. We'd both always wanted to be missionaries. We could quit our jobs, work with missionaries all over the world, and come back and write about it. It sounded simple.

Lying in bed that night, it didn't seem simple. Not only did we lack the training, but we lacked the finances.

Stacy and I had met as graduate students in Italy. We completed our master's degrees in third world economic development at Johns Hopkins University in Washington, D.C., and fell in love with the city. My first job was on Capitol Hill. I now had a great position with a telecommunications corporation. I was even up for a promotion.

Stacy had worked for a while resettling refugees for World Relief. Now she managed East Coast inner-city services for the Christian Broadcasting Network.

We had traveled in over 20 countries, worked in outreach projects in Central and South America, and served on our church's mission board. We thought we could handle anything.

_____

We were at this final gathering of friends when the enormity of what we were about to do began to set in.

Stacy and I had many things in common, including each being the oldest of four children. But we were complete opposites in appearance.

Stacy was a slender blonde with a pixie face and devilish blue eyes. Even with heels on, her eyes were about level with my chin. A dedicated extrovert, she loved to play sports, and found it impossible to sit still.

I was thin, too, but no one would describe me as petite. I had dark brown eyes; dark, naturally curly hair; and a generous supply of freckles (which I tried to cover with powder) across the bridge of my nose. To me, fun was cuddling up for hours with a good book.

Stacy was explaining what we'd be doing for the next 14 months. "We start in the Philippines at a conference for more than 2,000 missionaries. Then we'll go to Asia for about eight months, then to the Middle East, Europe, and

Central America. Twenty countries in all.

"We wrote YWAM bases in all these countries to find out exactly what they do. They'll house and feed us for most of the trip, and allow us to work with them as much as possible. In one country, we'll be working with refugees; in another, with drug addicts. In some, we'll pass out tracts on street corners."

"Then we'll write a book about it when we get back," I added.

Everyone seemed properly impressed.

"Aren't you scared?" a friend asked hesitantly.

"Scared?" We looked at each other. "Should we be?"

Stacy made it sound as if everything had just fallen into place. Actually, this trip was the culmination of months of planning and research.

Once we decided to work exclusively with YWAM, we got a list of key bases around the world. We wrote almost 30 of them, asking for permission to be housed on base and work alongside their missionaries. We also asked for the cost of staying there and traveling within their country.

We couldn't believe it when all of them encouraged us to come and even suggested the best time. We drew up an itinerary and wrote back to confirm our arrival dates. We decided to go to the major base in each country and let the staff there arrange for us to visit other bases in the country.

The best airfare we found was $3,100. From information supplied by YWAM bases and budget travel books, we figured in an additional $500 per month for meals and lodging, transportation not covered by our plane tickets, health insurance, and incidentals. Film and developing would cost a lot, but we had to keep a record of our trip.

All totaled, we each needed $10,000. It might as well have been ten million.

First we threw in our life savings. Our church's missions board granted us some support. Then we spoke at

Bible study groups and to any group that showed even a slight interest. Slowly, pledges began to come in.

Next we set up joint accounts at our parents' banks where the pledge money, channeled through our church, could be deposited. We had our mail forwarded to our parents so they could pay our monthly bills. We would draw cash advances on our credit cards.

We didn't make our budget goal, but we each started out with a plane ticket, $2000 in the bank, and a lot of faith.

I remember the day I sat in my room staring at the assorted piles that comprised my life. A treasured photo album from high school, a bouquet of silk flowers from my sister's wedding, a floral scarf my father had brought me from China. A stack of business suits and fancy dresses lay on the bed: I wouldn't need them. A stuffed animal leaned against my pillow: no room for him. I measured the backpack and carryon that had to hold 14 months of belongings. Tears rolled down my cheeks.

Stacy bounced into the room. "I finished packing," she chirped. "Have you?"

"Not yet." I glared at her. "I got sidetracked."

Stacy seemed incapable of understanding how I felt. Everything was an adventure to her. She kept reminding me that we'd be back in a year. But in my heart, there was a finality to our leaving. Even if we came back here, it would never be the same. I mourned the passing of a certain way of life.

"Here, I'll help," Stacy offered. Working quickly, she gathered up the scattered travel guides, note pads, tape recorder, blank tapes, water purifying tablets, and medications to thwart off every imaginable rare disease. Then she tackled my closet. She eliminated all the winter clothes, since we'd primarily be in tropical climates.

"Too hot for jeans," she insisted, setting them aside. "Too many shirts. You only need five or six. Take some that dry fast and don't wrinkle."

She reduced my stack of T-shirts in half, and added cotton slacks, skirts, low-heeled shoes, and underwear. I lay on the bed, staring at the ceiling while she stuffed it all into my backpack and bundled the things I was leaving behind in cardboard cartons.

With surgical precision, my life was stripped down to the barest essentials in a matter of minutes.

One of our housemates was taking us by a clinic for typhoid shots on our way to the airport. I didn't know how we'd make the plane on time. I had protested all along that waiting until the last minute for this shot was a bad idea, but Stacy didn't think it would be a problem. She never worried about details; I always did.

There was a long line at the clinic, as usual. Almost every Friday for the past two months, we'd stood in that line to get immunizations against diseases almost unknown in the United States. We were sure to be exposed to them along the way.

"Nanci Hogan. Stacy Sells."

We followed a nurse into a back room where she scanned our yellow immunization cards.

"I see you've had plenty of shots. That's good. Some countries won't let you in until you show them this card. They don't want anyone spreading diseases, and they don't want to be responsible if you catch something there."

"By the way, where are you going?"

Stacy began rattling off the places.

"Are you sure you're healthy enough?" The nurse looked at her apprehensively. "You're awfully thin. You need a good ten-pound cushion. One bout of dysentery will land you in the hospital."

I nodded my head vehemently. I'd been begging Stacy for weeks to gain some weight. A friend told me he'd lost 20 pounds in India when he got dysentery. I almost backed out of the trip at that point. I didn't know what I'd do if Stacy had a medical emergency.

"Several months ago, she got so dizzy she couldn't even finish walking around our block," I said knowingly to the nurse. "I had to go get a car and pick her up."

"She exaggerates," Stacy protested. "I do have low blood sugar, but if I stay away from sugar and caffeine, I'll be all right. I carry peanuts with me all the time in case I need a quick fix."

The nurse looked at me sympathetically. "When do you leave?"

"In an hour. We fly to the Philippines."

She gasped. "Isn't it dangerous there?"

"It can be," Stacy admitted. "But we're not worried."

———————————

At the airport, our housemate handed us each a rose and several sealed envelopes. "Don't read these until you're in the air," she said. "They're from people who couldn't be here."

I turned around as I entered the plane for a last look at the city I'd come to call home, and caught a glimpse of the Capitol bathed in the afternoon light. That's when I realized I had that funny little feeling back in my gut again, and it was growing.

When we opened our cards, checks and cash fell out.

"Stacy, almost all my cards have money in them."

"I know. So do mine."

"Everyone's been so generous. So many people are praying for us and supporting us. It's like a team effort."

"I don't know where the money for the rest of the trip will come from, but somehow we've had enough for each step so far," Stacy said.

———————————

When we changed planes in California, the flight attendant led us to the only two empty seats: center row in the middle of the smoking section. I tucked aspirin in the seat back in front of me; cigarette smoke always gave me a headache. And a little boy sat next to me. I was dreading this flight.

We lifted off and, just as I closed my eyes, a child started shrieking. As we reached cruising altitude, the seat belt sign was turned off. Two kids somewhere behind me started fighting, while others played tag down the aisle. The father of the boy to my right reached for an airsickness bag for his son. Too late.

Stacy was restless, so after a few minutes, she went to talk to one of the attendants. I leaned back and struggled to keep my composure. When we boarded the plane in Washington, I tried to prepare myself for the 37-1/2 hours and four plane changes before we got to Manila. Even then we would arrive late at night the day before the conference started. I tried to forget the television pictures I had glimpsed at the Los Angeles airport of the monsoon which was at this moment pelting the Philippines.

I didn't see how I'd ever make it. My head was already throbbing, but I thought a missionary should be smiling and uncomplaining.

I watched Stacy talking to the stewardess up by the galley. Her hands never stopped moving. I knew Stacy was probably telling her about our trip, trying to sneak in a way to talk to her about God. She was always looking for an opening.

I picked up the journal poking out of my carryon bag. I hadn't had time to write in it for weeks. There was one event I didn't want to forget to record.

In the frenzy of last-minute preparations, we felt as though we'd lost touch with God, and wondered if we were following His will or ours. We prayed about what He wanted us to do, but it seemed that God was silent. As it turned out, we almost missed hearing His answer.

Tired of goodbyes and overwhelmed by last-minute errands, we almost canceled our lunch with Belta, an Ethiopian refugee we'd befriended over the years.

Our Bible study group sponsored Belta and her cousin when they came to the United States. The group's responsibilities ended with finding them a home, ensuring their medical care, and helping them get a job, but Stacy and I remained their friends. Now the proud owner of two hot dog stands, Belta begged us to come for lunch.

There was already a crowd of young professionals and government workers lined up when we arrived. Belta, a tiny woman with creamy brown skin and luminous black eyes, beamed when she saw us.

She prepared our hot dogs, and motioned toward an empty spot on the sidewalk for us to sit down. When the crowds thinned, she joined us, entertaining us with humorous observations of American culture as we ate.

When Belta got up to serve a customer, I turned to Stacy.

"Her English has improved so much."

"I know. It's hard to believe she barely spoke a word of it three years ago."

When she returned, Stacy asked her, "Belta, what time do you start work in the morning?"

"I pick up my hot dog stands at 5:00 in the morning and bring them here. I have to get here early or someone will take my spot. It's, how you Americans say, 'first come, first served.'"

"Do you work year 'round?" I asked.

"Yes."

"Even in the winter?"

She nodded.

"It's worse in the summer. It gets so humid. But I like it. Sometimes if people don't have enough money to buy a hot dog, I give them one. I remember how the American nurses in the refugee camps used to feed me when I was sick. In fact, I want to be a nurse. I've been studying at the university part-time."

I shook my head. By my calculations, she was already on her feet 12 hours a day at the stand. I didn't know how she found the time or the energy. She looked small and fragile with her high cheekbones and delicate features, but she had great inner strength. This woman had known suffering. After fleeing persecution from the Marxist government in Ethiopia, she'd spent years in a refugee camp in Sudan, cut off from family and friends. It was hard to believe that she was only 22.

As we rose to leave, she gave us each a couple of twenty-dollar bills. "These are for the book." That was how she referred to our mission. "If you have any problems or run out of money, just let me know."

After our talk with Belta, I was awake much of that night thinking about her. Then it hit me. The purpose of our trip was to make a difference in lives wherever we went, and to leave behind an example of loving service and a desire to know the Lord.

The seat belt warning light flashed on as we hit a pocket of turbulence. I'd just finished my journal observations. The fighting children had fallen asleep, and Stacy was back in her seat, reading her Bible. All was right with the world.

I closed the journal, certain that God had some great things ahead for us. If only I could know what would be written on those blank pages in a year.

Reaching out my hand, I ruffled the hair of the little boy next to me. This flight hadn't been so bad after all.

2

Jungle Boot Camp (Stacy)

We were smug and confident when we set out to change the world. It was 7:30 a.m., and I shifted from one foot to the other as we waited for the Dangwa bus to the tribal villages of the northern Philippines. We needed to reach Bontoc, 90 miles away, and the journey would take over nine hours.

It was August, height of the monsoon season, and we'd been warned that our way could be temporarily blocked by mud slides. We had also heard that buses frequently slipped off the one-lane dirt highway, only to disappear into the valley thousands of feet below. I shrugged off such dire possibilities. Most likely, we'd simply break down and be stranded.

We'd been warned to catch the first bus of the day, the one which left at 7:00 a.m. But we'd arrived late. Now, even the 8:00 a.m. bus was full. We waited with the crowd for the last bus of the day—the one which left at nine.

"When it comes, be ready to run and push your way in. There's never enough room for everyone," our Filipino hostess had warned us.

An old, no-frills vehicle pulled into the dirt lot, and everyone rushed to board it. Juggling all our luggage, we merged into the throng. We were lucky to find an empty bench near the front; otherwise, we would have had to stand up the entire trip or ride "top load" on the roof, penned in with chickens and pigs.

People, animals, assorted baggage, and parcels were

jammed into every conceivable space. Our feet were inches short of touching the floor with all the things we had to sit on. When nothing more could be stuffed inside or on top, the bus departed, looking like a rolling market. Women steadied sacks of beans and rice atop their heads. Spinach and cabbage leaves protruded from the windows, and chickens wove their way through a maze of legs, squawking their displeasure.

We limped and chugged up and around mountains, negotiating hairpin turns as we ascended. Pebbles skittered off the edge of the narrow road, disappearing into the dark void beyond.

Occasionally we had to wait for a bulldozer to clear a stretch where mud had formed an impassable wall. We often passed stalled vehicles. People banged on the sides of our bus and pled to be let on. We drove past one of the other Dangwa buses. It had broken down, and passengers were settling down to sleep, preparing for a long night on the road.

I quickly surmised that there were no roadside comfort stations. When a bathroom was needed, a passenger came forward, told the driver, and he stopped. Privacy was highly respected. No one watched when an individual left the bus. Several times, the driver called for an "official" potty stop. Then everyone got off. Women went to the left and men to the right.

Eventually we stopped for lunch at a roadside shack. The man ahead of me ordered dog stew, but I balked at eating "man's best friend," and settled for rice.

The stop gave me time to observe my fellow travelers. Many were from mountain tribes. The older men wore traditional tribal garb of colorful G-strings, with large knives tucked in their waists. Since they had no pockets, handwoven purses dangled from their necks. Tattoos on the chests of the older men designated how many heads they had taken. When American military advisors entered the mountains in World War II, they taught the headhunting tribes to settle disputes in a more peaceful manner.

After lunch, we squeezed back into our seats and for five more hours, we dipped up and down through pond-size potholes, in and out of cloud banks, until it grew nearly dark. Finally we entered the frontier town of Bontoc, stopping right in front of the mission house.

"You're here!" the base director, Jacqui, rushed out to greet us. "We've been worried. This is the first bus that's made it from Baguio today."

I recalled that we had seen only one by the side of the road. The other...I didn't want to think about it.

We had come to Bontoc specifically to meet this woman. Jacqui Schori had pioneered a YWAM work in these remote mountains nine years earlier. Now she had a team of ten people planting churches among the animist tribes.

Jacqui had arranged to take us to some of the villages where she first began. I studied her as she gave us a bit of background. She tucked her long, blonde hair behind her ears, and stretched her legs to rest on a chair in front of her. Being Swiss, she was strong and sturdy, an interesting contrast to the dark-haired, coal-eyed, slight Filipinos she worked among.

She had been a YWAMer in Manila when her leader persuaded her to join a team in these mountains to show the Christian film *The Cross and the Switchblade*.

"One night, after we'd shown the movie, a man stood up and said he wanted to know more. He wondered whom he could talk to after we left.

"His unanswered question haunted me," Jacqui said. "Finally, one Sunday morning, I said, 'Okay, Lord, if You want me to work with mountain tribes, tell me today.'

"That morning at church, I was almost relieved when the minister announced he would be speaking from Song of Solomon. *There aren't any mountain passages in that book,* I thought to myself. Then suddenly, he stopped in the middle of the sermon. He asked the congregation to open their Bibles to Isaiah 52:7, from which he read: 'How beautiful on the mountains are the feet of those who bring good news.' He stopped there, put down his Bible, and returned to his sermon.

"I began crying. I knew I was moving to the mountains."

The first three years, Jacqui lived in the isolated town of Abatan with two Filipino nurses. "They were my teachers. It was a hard time for me," her voice softened. "The hardest part was seeing my own shortcomings.

"I had to change from the inside out. To be effective in this work, you have to be totally broken; you have to die to Western culture, and become as Asian as possible.

"That's enough," she stopped abruptly. "I want you to meet the people." As we walked out, she added, "I hope you can adjust. The last ones couldn't."

"What's that?" Jacqui asked, pointing to the two bags we carried into her house.

"Our luggage," I grinned. We had taken all the "necessary" items out of our large backpacks and put them into medium-sized soft suitcases so we could travel lightly.

"Much too big." She went into her room and came out with two small daypacks. "We'll only be gone five days."

I was hurt. I thought we'd pared down to the essentials. I repacked one pair of long pants, two shirts, clean underwear, a toothbrush, hairbrush, camera, micro-cassette recorder, and Pepto Bismol. A plastic water bottle hung from my daypack's outside loop. With bandannas around our necks and mirrored shades covering our eyes, we headed out. My ego was still bruised.

As we left for Abatan, I decided to get to know Pascual, the young Filipino who was to be our escort for the trip. I reached back and tapped his shoulder to get his attention.

Instinctively, he jumped and started to throw a punch at me. My touch was meant as a playful gesture; his was not. I was shocked, and turned around in my seat. Jacqui had seen what happened. She leaned over and quietly explained that Filipino men and women never touch one another in public.

We stopped in three villages before reaching our destination for the night. Two families shared the small, wooden home where we were hosted. Dinner was served by kerosene lamp and interrupted by Nanci's shriek as a four-inch cockroach landed on her plate. (Later a gecko, an Asian lizard, plopped onto her head during prayer time.)

By bedtime, I was thoroughly stuffed, exhausted, and worried. Never had I consumed so many sodas in one day. We had been given one at each of our stops, and it would have been rude to refuse. I spent a fitful night shifting from side to side on the wooden board that served as my bed. Sitting up, I finally came to grips with my greatest fear: that my health wouldn't hold out. Since I'd always brushed off the subject with Nanci, I couldn't bring it up now. I'd have to deal with it alone.

Then I realized that something incredible had happened: the sugar I'd had in all those sodas today hadn't affected me at all.

I awoke to whispers in the next room.

"I think they'll do it," I heard Jacqui say. At breakfast, I found out what "it" was.

"The school's principal came by this morning and asked if you girls would speak to the sixth-grade English class. They understand English pretty well, and are learning about different parts of the United States."

"Great," I responded quickly. We'd done so much listening that I jumped at the chance to talk.

When we entered the classroom, all heads turned. The children were from outlying villages. They attended school five days a week, lived in dorms, and hiked back to their homes on weekends. Their parents sacrificed for them to get an education; the family missed the extra hands in the fields.

The school's walls were made of bamboo poles held together by vine ropes. There were no doors, just openings on two sides through which stray dogs and chickens ambled. There were no blackboards, books, or teaching supplies. No file cabinets or cafeterias. No amenities whatsoever. Each child was given a note pad of flimsy grayish-white paper and a ballpoint pen. That was all.

"Welcome," the teacher said, graciously bowing her head. Each child rose in unison, turned to face us, placed a hand over his heart, and in perfect English, recited the Pledge of Allegiance to the flag of the United States.

Nanci went first, drawing a crude map of the United States on a large pad of paper the teacher handed her. She pointed to where Pennsylvania, her home state, was located, and described the steel industry it was famous for. She was met with blank stares. None of them had ever heard of Pennsylvania, let alone the steel industry.

My job was easier since I was from California. I told them about Hollywood, Disneyland, beaches, and mountains. They knew about movies, because people like Jacqui's team came to their village from time to time with generators and screens and showed movies. I told the students that one of California's biggest crops was rice, and they were delighted to learn that rice grew in other places besides their villages.

We thanked them for inviting us, and were preparing to leave when the teacher stopped us. "Wait," she said, "we have a surprise for you."

The students rose again. Ivory smiles lit their brown faces. The teacher led them through all the verses of "America the Beautiful." (I never knew there were so many.) When they sang, "God shed His grace on thee," I began to cry. God had most certainly shed His grace on me, and I softly prayed He would do the same for them.

The following days were much like the first. Soon we were traversing lofty rice terraces like veterans, negotiating the stair steps as if walking a balance beam. To slip off the narrow borders meant falling into muddy rice patches. We were slow at the beginning, but by our fourth afternoon, we were able to cross the treacherous terraces all the way to the tiny village of Duc-Duc.

As we walked, I talked to Pascual. He often darted ahead, leaping obstacles like a gazelle, then quietly circling back to jump from behind a bush and scare us.

"How did you become a church worker?" I asked.

For the next half hour, he shared about his wild teenage years. He'd been shot twice. Once they thought he'd surely die, but he was "tough," as he said. He pulled through.

"When I became a Christian three years ago, I quit all that stuff. It was hard at first, and I made a lot of mistakes, but God never let me down. Now, all I want to do is share my story in the villages I grew up in."

"Hello!" shouted a woman in a field below us. She dropped her hoe and ran to greet us. Elisa was Duc-Duc's first Christian, and leader of the village's tiny church.

"We've been waiting for you," she said.

"Communication in the mountains is almost as good as by telephone," Jacqui had told us. Apparently this was true, for everyone we met had heard we were coming, and was waiting for us.

Continuing around the mountain, we saw tiny, straw huts and one small, wooden platform with a corrugated metal roof. Elisa's place. That evening, Elisa cooked for us, her son, and the hundreds of flies that blanketed our food. Our meal was interrupted several times by knocks at the door. Recent, enthusiastic converts stopped by to talk about their new faith. I marveled at the work of God in this isolated village.

In this part of the world, time was anchored by the rise and fall of the sun. We awoke at sunrise; we went to bed when it got dark. I had long since shed my watch, since there was no use for it.

"There's a shower outside, girls," said Elisa, handing us a worn towel to share.

I walked around the house, looking for the shower room. I saw nothing. The second time around, I bumped into Jacqui coming up the hill.

"Elisa sent us outside to shower, but I can't find it," I said.

She smiled and led me to a clothesline. Hanging over the line was a hose, its nozzle arched in such a way that it looked like a shower head. *Nanci will love this,* I thought, calling her to join me.

"I found it."

"No way." Her eyes grew huge.

"Yeah, we can do it. I'll keep an eye out for you, and you do the same for me."

Nanci went first, taking the quickest shower of her life.

When we got back to the house, Elisa was sitting on the front steps with her son. She picked through his scalp methodically, flicking aside lice. We'd slept in his bed the night before.

Elisa served a breakfast of sardines, boiled spinach, and coffee. "Do they know about *tingao*?" she asked Jacqui.

Elisa bent toward us and lowered her voice.

"*Tingao* is a religious practice which shuts down all village activity. It's declared without warning by one of the seers, whenever he determines the gods are upset. No one is allowed to enter or leave the village during this time. Anyone violating a *tingao* is killed."

"How do you know when one's in progress and when it will be over?" I asked, suddenly quite interested in the subject.

"At the entrance to the village, rocks and branches are stacked in a certain way to signify that a *tingao* is in progress. It can last up to two weeks."

Jacqui chimed in, "The corpses of three tourists who defied a *tingao* were recently unearthed. I was trapped in a village during one. It lasted so long that I missed my flight home to Switzerland."

We listened to Elisa's stories for hours. As we left, I overheard Jacqui saying to her, "I'm so proud of them. They've never once asked for a toilet, and they eat anything." Those words meant as much as an "A" on any exam I had ever taken.

After three hours of hiking uphill, Pascual leading the way and the hot sun beating down on our weary bodies, we arrived at the edge of our last village, Malingcong.

Jacqui suddenly stopped. She stared at a precise stack of rocks and branches on the ground. *Tingao!*

She walked slowly around the pile, bending down to study it carefully. "It's okay," she reassured us. "This means a low *tingao,* not a high one. We can enter for a short time, but can't spend the night."

I didn't remember Elisa saying anything about high and low *tingaos.* I did remember men with tattooed chests, sharp machetes, and stories of missing tourists.

Boldly, Jacqui marched in. Obediently, we followed.

3

Run for Your Lives (Stacy)

An elderly man walked toward us as we approached a cluster of wooden huts. His bare feet shuffling on the dirt path was the only sound except my pounding heart.

Jacqui stepped forward and greeted him in a tribal dialect. I smiled cautiously. No tattoos—a good sign.

He bowed and muttered a few words.

"It's fine," Jacqui whispered. "We can stay a few hours, as long as we leave in time to reach Bontoc before dark. The government has set curfews for this area."

Guerrilla activity had escalated. Several killings had been reported in neighboring villages. Military choppers awakened us each morning, and we heard machine gun strafing all day, every day, in the distance.

We walked through a maze of homes stacked like card houses on top of one another. Their inhabitants blended into shadowy doorways, children clinging to parents' legs, a few daring to wave.

News of our arrival spread quickly, and Barb came to join us. She was an American YWAMer who lived and worked in Malingcong. She looked as strong and sturdy as most of the women in these farming communities.

As we walked, Barb told us that she had moved to Malingcong a year earlier to learn the language and customs of the people. The villagers worshiped pagan gods and followed elaborate rituals to appease the gods.

"Every morning, I walk with an elderly woman to the rice fields," Barb said. "She can't stand up straight anymore—too many years of bending over the fields. I can only work three or four hours before my muscles get too sore to continue. She stays all day.

"I spend as much time as I can with the people. I do my laundry in the river and collect wood for cooking. I go to the markets in nearby villages to buy food.

"I haven't told them yet why I'm here. I need to earn the right to do that. God will show me the time and person to reveal myself to."

She knew the importance of building relationships first in missions work. But how could Barb explain to her donors that she'd spent a year living in this village without once preaching a sermon, holding a Bible study, or passing out a tract? Would they understand? Did I?

"This is the village elder's house," Barb said, stopping. "He wanted to meet you as soon as you arrived. It's *tingao,* you know, but he allowed you to enter anyway."

An old man appeared at the top of the stairs, wearing the typical embroidered G-string that I had become accustomed to seeing. He motioned to us, and we followed Jacqui and Barb up a wooden ladder.

As we entered, we introduced ourselves, bowed, and took seats on the floor. Our circle included Jacqui, Barb, Pascual, Nanci, myself, and the "chief." Barb did the translating.

"He would like you to have a meal with him."

Jacqui answered quickly, "We are honored."

So it was settled. Nanci and I nodded agreement.

The chief's house was about the size of a walk-in closet. In one corner was a rope bed with a thick wool blanket on top. In another corner, a circle of rocks defined the cooking area. Wood was burned within the circle, with the smoke escaping through a hole in the ceiling straight above it. The walls were blackened from years of smoke that failed to make it out the hole. The rest of the room was empty.

Jacqui and Barb quit talking when they noticed a servant gingerly climbing the ladder, juggling a number of steaming hot pots.

Even being a rookie missionary, I knew it was important to eat whatever food was offered. Nanci and I had already managed to down a dog and some unidentifiable dishes, but I knew we were in for a new experience when I glanced in the pots.

Jacqui helped herself first. Relieved, I saw that it was rice. I took a generous portion. The second pot was passed. Peering inside, I paled at the sight of pig tails, intestines, and skin—black bristles and all—swimming in a greasy broth. Like Russian roulette, I closed my eyes and dropped the ladle into the stew, scooping out my catch. I poured a spoonful of hair and skin on top of my mound of rice.

As Jacqui handed the third and final pot to me, she winked encouragingly. Inside was a collection of snails. Not the sort found in fancy French restaurants bathed in garlic butter, but the variety that trailed across front lawns at home.

"How do you eat these?" I whispered to Jacqui, afraid I would have to crunch the thing with my teeth.

"Put them to your mouth and suck," she said, demonstrating the technique. "The body comes right out and the shell is thrown on the floor."

After the meal, the chief had one more thing to say to us. Barb translated his words. She began humbly, "He wants you to know that he considers me as one of his daughters. He says I am one of the village." Later, she told us that this was the first confirmation she had received from the villagers.

We said our goodbyes and started down the hill for the three-hour hike to Bontoc. Jacqui reminded us again of the urgency to get back before nightfall. The guerrillas moved at night, and the route between Malingcong and Bontoc was one of their favorites.

I caught up with Jacqui. "Why were the village people so timid?" I asked.

"They're afraid. The guerrillas steal their money, houses, and food; they burn crops and rape women. They kill anyone who resists. The people don't know whether to get guns and try to fight them, or just hope their village will be passed by."

I understood the need to keep a low profile. Since we were white, we could be taken for spies, and kidnapped or killed. We moved quickly and quietly, not speaking to or establishing eye contact with anyone we passed. We were anxious to reach the relative safety of Bontoc, the military headquarters for the area. We arrived just as night fell.

One night, Nanci and I offered to prepare dinner for Jacqui's team members, who were mostly Filipinos. We decided to fix chicken and stir fry vegetables. With rice, of course. Jacqui said chicken would be a real treat. It was much more expensive than pig or dog.

Lacking the conveniences of a modern kitchen, we began as soon as lunch dishes were cleaned up. For hours we scrubbed, chopped, sliced, and peeled a huge array of vegetables and cooked them *al dente*. We carefully pulled all the skin off the chicken.

In the midst of our preparation, Jacqui came to tell us that about 20 extra people might join us. "They're a family visiting Bontoc for a funeral, and I invited them to come for dinner and to watch a movie," she said. We ran out and bought more of everything.

At six o'clock we rang the dinner bell.

The staff lined up with bowls and spoons. I savored the taste of chicken and vegetables that crunched instead of mushed.

Everyone complimented us on the meal. But as one of the men went to wash his bowl, he spied the mound of chicken skins we had set aside for the trash. He called some other Filipinos over. They were delighted with their find, and immediately scooped lard into a frying pan and fried the skins, eating them like candy.

Jacqui explained that the skin was the most sought-after part of the chicken, and that firm vegetables were strange to them.

"They think they're not cooked if they make a noise when you eat them."

We apologized for not having done better research, and vowed never to make the same mistake again. While they fried the skins, Nanci and I steamed the remaining vegetables until they were limp.

An hour later, there was a knock at the door. The other group had arrived for dinner. It didn't matter that there weren't enough bowls or spoons; they ate with their hands, returning again and again until every grain of rice was gone. Our dinner party was a success after all.

After dinner, we decided to take advantage of the joys of electricity. Everyone sat on the cement floor and watched an old movie on a video that a donor had mailed to one of the team. I noticed how engrossed the team was. Every eye was locked on the tiny black and white TV screen.

"I didn't know they spoke English," I said to Jacqui.

"They don't," she replied. "They just like watching the pictures."

They sat for three hours. Sometimes they laughed; sometimes they seemed on the verge of tears. Who knew what impression they were getting of American life.

———————

It had been ten days since our arrival in Bontoc. The staff was planning a going-away party for us, complete with homemade pizza and cinnamon rolls prepared by Barb, who had hiked in to see us off. We would leave early the next morning for another mountain province.

Paulina, one of the YWAMers who worked with Jacqui,

asked us to accompany her to the village of Belili. She, too, was leaving the next day for a year of Bible training, and wanted to say goodbye to special friends. Paulina was very comfortable with the Filipinos' disregard for time, but that day, it was really causing us problems.

We followed Paulina in and out of huts as she said her goodbyes. With each farewell, we were handed things like sweet potatoes, carrots, and cabbage. Before long, each of us had accumulated a large, heavy bag of gifts.

Jacqui had repeatedly warned us not to miss the last bus back to Bontoc, the one which left at 6:00. To do so would mean being stuck in rebel territory at night. I had put my watch back on for this excursion.

As the sun lowered in the sky, Nanci and I grew increasingly alarmed.

"We need to leave now!" I insisted, tugging at Paulina.

"Just a few more stops," she said. "The buses never leave on time."

It was a treacherously steep 20-minute walk down the mountainside to the bus stop. What's more, it had begun to rain. Now the path was muddy and even harder to navigate.

Nanci and I ran as fast as we dared, half dragging our heavy burdens. We weren't saying a word to Paulina at this point. Slipping and sliding, we grabbed branches to anchor us on the steep, muddy grade. We reached the bus stop just as darkness and rain dealt their heaviest blows.

By seven o'clock, even Paulina acknowledged that we had missed the bus. The night was totally black except for an obscure beam of moonlight. There was no hope of making our way back up the trail to Belili in the dark.

Paulina suggested we start walking in the direction of Bontoc, 15 miles away, in hopes that someone friendly might drive by and offer us a ride. Chances were slim, she acknowledged. The roadway itself had numerous hazardous switchbacks through the mountains, dangerous even in daylight. No one with any sense would be out on that road at night. Except rebels.

We walked down the middle of the road. To calm our nerves, we feebly chanted the familiar words from *The Wizard of Oz*, "Lions and tigers and bears, oh, my!" Then we fell silent, realizing we might draw attention to ourselves by making any noise.

The rain hitting the leaves sounded like footsteps running toward us. We saw the faint glow of headlights approaching in the distance. We decided to take our chances and flag down the vehicle rather than risk a night in the jungle.

As it drew nearer, my heart sank. It was too late to hide. The rowdy, disheveled men filling the elongated jeep had seen us, and they were slowing down. We eyed each other.

Paulina stepped forward to speak, since she knew the local dialect. Her face was strangely taut as she turned back to face us. "I think it's all right," she said softly.

Nanci and I huddled on one of the bench seats that ran the length of both sides of the jeep. We sat as close to the back as possible. Paulina stood outside on the back running board, holding on for dear life.

I looked away, pretending not to notice as the men inspected me from head to toe. Without warning, we turned off the main road and headed up a tiny dirt one that wound around the mountain.

"I'm worried," I managed to stutter the understatement of my life to Paulina. "Just pray," she said.

After a few minutes, I asked her what they were saying. Instead of answering me, she jumped off the back of the moving jeep and began running downhill, frantically screaming for help. I decided it was time to bail out, too. I stood up, closed my eyes, and leaped into the darkness. Hands reached out and pulled me back. The more they pulled, the harder I fought. I broke free and fell to the ground. The jeep continued to race up the hill.

Nanci flew out next. All three of us were running and screaming wildly down the hill, shedding our sandals as we ran.

A safe distance away, Paulina stopped and began to cry. "Maybe we should have trusted them," she wavered. "Now they're going to really be mad and come looking for us." I suggested that we find a hiding place in the bushes and wait out the night. Nanci, on the other hand, thought we might have misjudged them and should apologize and get back in if they returned.

Within ten minutes, they did return, this time with a lot fewer men. Heads hung low and shivering in the cold, we waited desperately beside the road. The driver told Paulina that they had dropped the others off at a camp and were now heading for Bontoc. We didn't ask what type of camp it was. We didn't want to know. We climbed back in the jeep. When we saw the lights of Bontoc in the distance, we took our first deep breaths.

Wet, muddy, hungry, and still shaking, we walked into the mission house. The others had held our going-away party without us, and most of the food was gone.

Pascual rushed over and told us how worried he'd been. After helping gather up the remaining food for us to devour, he listened as we tearfully related each frightening detail of the past several hours.

———————

Note: Two months later, Pascual was accidentally shot and killed. He was in a village discipling a group of new believers. The tragedy of his death opened up opportunities to share the Gospel with hundreds who attended his funeral and heard of God for the first time.

4

Ladies in Waiting (Nanci)

Stacy wasn't her effervescent self when she returned from the ticket counter at the airport in Singapore.

"They took the first four on the waiting list; we were numbers five and six. The next flight to Beijing is in five days. And we're wait-listed on it," she said. "The ticket agent suggested we fly to Hong Kong and then take a train into southern China."

"We can't afford another night in a hotel," I protested.

"I've got the name of some friends of my parents who live here. Maybe they'll put us up for a few days; it's our only hope."

I paced up and down while Stacy phoned them. After much prayer a few weeks ago, we'd felt led to spend an extra ten days in the Philippines, even though it meant missing a confirmed flight to Beijing via Singapore. When we arrived in Singapore last night, we just knew that God would reward us by opening up two seats on this morning's overbooked flight. We were wrong.

"They were home," Stacy said, grinning. "Their driver's on his way."

An elegant Japanese car pulled up to the curb a few minutes later. A uniformed man hopped out and held the door open for us. Driving into downtown Singapore, we noted that the streets were spotless and the city sparkled as the early morning sun bounced from one huge plate glass window to another. A city bus stopped alongside us, and I saw lanes of expensive imported vehicles reflected in its highly polished side.

Strangely, I felt keenly disappointed. I had hoped for something more exotic, or at least more Asian. We could have been anywhere in the Western world, were it not for all the Chinese and Malay faces and, I suddenly noticed, the absence of litter and graffiti.

"Look at that sign," Stacy pointed out. "It says, 'Spitting is forbidden. Spitters will be fined.'"

We pulled up in front of a luxury highrise a block away from a row of five-star hotels. The driver led us inside to an elevator and pressed the penthouse button.

When we entered the apartment, my mouth fell open. I walked straight across to the opposite wall—a bank of floor-to-ceiling windows overlooking the city's skyline. Cathedral ceilings, white plush carpeting, and mirrored walls emphasized the spaciousness of the room. White linen furniture, peach and turquoise floral pillows, and glass-topped tables made it look like a picture straight out of a decorating magazine.

Our hostess led us to a corner bedroom with attached bath and introduced us to their *amah* (maid) who was told to take care of our every need. She then excused herself to let us unpack.

Stacy emerged from the bathroom wrapped in a long sheath of white terry cloth with a sheepish grin on her face. "You've gotta see this," she said, sweeping open the door.

The bathroom was white marble and brass. A sunken tub was surrounded on three sides by curved windows and had a view that rivaled that of the living room. The ocean shimmered on the horizon in the background.

Only a few hours earlier, we had almost resigned ourselves to sleeping on a park bench. We unpacked in stunned silence.

We found the *amah* ironing in the kitchen. While we visited, she worked with a fierce diligence, and only came alive when she spoke of her native Philippines.

"We just came from there," Stacy announced proudly. "It's so beautiful. How could you ever leave it?"

"There's no work. I'm a schoolteacher, but I couldn't get a job. My husband's here, too. We had to leave our children behind, and we can't even live together. We each live with the family we work for."

"Is that common?" I asked.

"All over Singapore and Hong Kong."

The city bus was new and air-conditioned, not what we were accustomed to. The aisles were empty; no one rode atop the bus, and no one carried live animals or produce.

"Everything's too sterile here. I don't like it," Stacy snapped.

We got off in the middle of town. I was anxious to explore; however, Stacy had that determined look on her face that I'd come to dread. She pulled a piece of paper from her purse.

"I made a list of TTDs," she said.

I rolled my eyes. Stacy was notorious for her TTD (Things To Do) lists. I braced myself.

"First, we'll go to the airline office and see if we can fly into Hong Kong instead of Beijing. Then we'll go to the American Express office and get some more traveler's checks. Then to the Thai and Indian embassies to get our visas, and then...."

"Wait a minute. Why do we need those visas now? We can get them when we return in two months."

"We have extra time today. Let's get it out of the way."

"But I don't want to spend the whole day running errands."

I wanted to visit the old Raffles Hotel, a haunt for authors who wrote about the romantic Orient of the Colonial Era. I'd heard that the hotel still looked the same: lounges with tiger heads and other exotic game mounted on the walls, ceiling fans, and rattan furniture. The Singapore Sling drink had originated here at the Raffles Hotel's famous long, caned bar.

But Stacy persisted and finally won out. We waited almost an hour at the airline office before we could even speak with anyone. The woman who finally assisted us stared at our tickets in confusion. She said she had never heard of an around-the-world ticket before. She called the manager. He was as perplexed as she. He faxed the United States. Once okayed, it took another hour to rewrite our entire tickets by hand. All just in case we decided to go to Hong Kong. My patience with TTDs was running short.

Long lines of visa applicants crisscrossed the room at the Indian embassy. We struggled to read the print on the form, barely decipherable on thin, gray paper. A large fan circulated hot air, and threatened to rearrange stacks of paper piled atop every counter and desk. Everyone seemed to passively accept the situation, so I tried to do the same.

After half an hour, three people had been helped.

"Let's go," I exploded. "We'll be here all day."

"We've waited this long; we might as well stay."

We discussed the pros and cons until we were in a full-blown argument that had more to do with our personality differences than anything else.

The louder I became, the quieter Stacy became. Finally I said, "I've had it. I'm sick of your Things To Do. You can wait here forever if you want, but I'm outta here."

I could feel the hair rising on the back of my neck as I marched out. A roomful of resigned eyes watched me go.

I went to the Raffles Hotel alone, and spent a leisurely afternoon window-shopping and people-watching, trying not to think about the fight we'd had.

When I got back to the apartment, Stacy was waiting. After a few tears and hugs, we agreed that forgiveness was an important part of so much togetherness. And Stacy admitted what had been on her mind.

"I'm so discouraged. China is a total question mark.

We don't even know exactly which cities we'll go to. I called, and we're still on standby for Beijing. I'm anxious to go witnessing."

That chance came sooner than we expected.

In the small, dimly lit restaurant, a haze of smoke obscured the jazz band we had come to hear. Worn, wooden tables were pushed closely together, and the only vacant one was next to two men. We sat down, ordered something to eat, and began to discuss what we hoped to accomplish in China.

"I hope we're as lucky as Pat," Stacy said. "When she was there, she met a lot of people interested in Christianity." Pat was a former housemate who had done a short-term mission in China, and was now a full-time missionary in Pakistan. We planned to visit her later in our trip.

As we talked, one of the men next to us leaned over. "Excuse me. I couldn't help noticing that you're fellow Americans. I'm a doctor. I've been working in Indonesia. Could we buy you a drink?"

"You can buy us dessert," Stacy offered.

They drew their chairs closer. The doctor wore a boldly flowered cotton shirt that yelled of tourist. It was draped tightly over his trousers in an effort to disguise years of overeating. His companion was tall, reed thin, and dressed in a dark business suit. He appeared embarrassed.

"What are you ladies doing overseas?" the doctor asked.

"We're missionaries," Stacy replied proudly.

At that, the doctor launched into a tirade while his companion looked on apologetically.

"Missionaries!" he spat. "Every missionary I met in Indonesia was either alcoholic or suicidal. They lived in big houses with lots of servants.

"Why do you want to mess with somebody's religion? One's as good as another. You Christians are so narrow-minded. I suppose you think that if I don't believe in Jesus, I'm going to hell."

Stacy drew in a deep breath. "Well, that's what the Bible says. And I believe the Bible is God's word. But," she hurried on, "I can't judge your heart. Only God can."

His face grew red and he slammed his fist to the table.

"I'm better than any missionary I've ever met. At least I try to help people. What do you do to help? Teaching them about your Jesus won't put food on their tables or clothes on their backs, will it? Get out of here!"

The room had suddenly grown quiet. Everyone was staring at us, and we were too shocked to respond or move.

"What are you waiting for?" he yelled even louder. "I said to get out!"

We sat in silence on the metro back to our penthouse suite, having failed miserably in an opportunity to witness. I wondered if I would be up to the task ahead.

Stacy and I sat in the packed airport cafeteria, eating breakfast, thumbing through the paper, and listening to the loud speaker give out flight information. I glanced over my shoulder at the clock on the wall. It was 7:00 a.m., and the flight to Beijing left at 9:50. We'd arrived early, and had moved to number one and two on standby.

"Why don't you go check again," Stacy said. "I would, but I'm feeling a little dizzy after what I ate last night."

Suppressing an "I-told-you-so," I went to the counter. No change. The next flight to Beijing with empty seats was in two weeks. On a whim, I asked about flights to Hong Kong. There was one at 9:40. It had openings.

"You need to get your boarding passes for it by 9:00," the agent warned. "You still might make the Beijing flight, but we won't know until final call at 9:40. And all the later Hong Kong flights are booked."

My head was spinning with times. If we decided to take our chances on the Beijing flight, we risked not making either one. And being stuck in Singapore again.

I went back to the cafeteria to consult Stacy. Neither of us felt led about what to do. We decided to stick with our original plan and try for Beijing. Relentlessly, we watched the clock and took turns making trips to the counter.

Thirty minutes went by. Stacy came back to tell me that we were still on standby.

"I've prayed and prayed, and I don't know where we should go. I do know for sure that I don't want to stay in Singapore any longer," I said. "We're just wasting time."

By 8:30 we were no nearer a decision, and had only half an hour before we had to commit. We weighed the pros and cons once more. Stacy paced around the room.

"I don't care," she said when she came back. "You choose. But we have to let them know. Now."

I forced myself back to the counter. It was 8:50.

"You're still on the waiting list. What do you want to do?"

I hesitated.

"Lady," the agent snapped, "make up your mind. People are waiting." I turned around and saw a long line of angry people staring at me.

Suddenly, I had my answer.

When I returned to Stacy, there was fear in her eyes, and she was shaking. "I've had the worst pit in my stomach ever since you left," her words tumbled out. "Every time I thought about going to Beijing, my palms got sweaty. We can't get on that plane. Run. Change our tickets."

She paused for a breath. "What are you waiting for?"

I smiled and handed her the boarding passes. They were stamped: Hong Kong.

To this day, we're still not sure why we were so apprehensive. We never heard anything more about the flight we didn't take. God must have known something that we didn't.

5

The Moon is Not Round in China (Stacy)

The wind blowing against my face felt as steamy as a vaporizer's mist. I leaned over the ship's guardrail, and watched Hong Kong harbor fade into the night. Our stay had been brief and uneventful, but we knew we'd return. Right now we were concerned with what lay ahead. China.

Occasionally, a whistle sounded when our ship passed another one, and passengers waved excitedly to one another. We could hear the steady beat of rock-and-roll music signaling that our ship's disco was open for business. We headed downstairs to investigate.

The first room we came to was the dining room. I entered, more curious than hungry. At every table, large bowls of rice were rapidly disappearing. Conversations were noisy and animated.

Most of the diners were residents of China returning from shopping sprees. (Anyone who had relatives in Hong Kong could pay the Chinese government the equivalent of $400 for a week's visit to buy products unavailable in China. Judging from the enormous number of boxes and bags we had seen being loaded, everyone had enjoyed a very successful trip.)

Proceeding to our cabin, we were amazed at its comforts: air conditioning, bath slippers, and a thermos of hot tea. We later found out that tea was available anytime and anyplace in China.

While getting ready for bed, we talked about the success stories we had heard about China. A friend had been the guest of several families, spending days at different houses teaching from the Bible. A high government official had even been one of her students. Another friend had described sneaking around at night to visit underground churches. According to him, there were lots of them there.

Then I got right to the point.

"Nanci," I said, "aren't you worried about what we're taking into China?" I had been so nervous all day I could hardly eat; a rare thing for me.

"We've only got two Bibles apiece. That's legal."

I was about out of patience. She seemed to be in denial.

"Well, what about the bookmarks and Bible studies? Are you forgetting about them?

We were carrying 20 bookmarks with Chinese Bible verses. Also, we had 40 addressed envelopes containing Chinese Bible studies. We were to get them into the country, stamp them, and drop them into a mailbox. I had no idea what might happen to us if we were caught with them, let alone what might happen to the people they were addressed to. I didn't even want to think about it.

I could tell from the look on Nanci's face that she didn't want to talk about it. I could tell, too, that she was as scared as I was.

I turned out the light and tried to get some sleep. And I started praying really hard. Tomorrow we would wake up in Guangzhou.

The next morning, I tucked my head down and prayed all the way up to the customs agent, trying to avoid his eyes as I finally stood before him. He slowly looked us over and then passed us through, not noticing my sweaty palms and sigh of relief. I made sure that the first thing we did was to buy some stamps and get rid of the incriminating evidence.

Next we found the little booths set up to exchange money. In China there are actually two currencies. The FEC, legally only for the use of foreigners, is worth two or three times as much as the RMB, the money used by citizens. Yet FEC had to be used to purchase certain appliances and high-tech goods. We were not supposed to have any RMBs. But whenever we received change, it was given in RMBs. I never figured out the system.

I suggested going to bed early our first night in China since I had lost so much sleep the night before. I was really feeling edgy. Nanci and I both had a premonition that we might run into trouble from demonic forces somewhere along the way. We even talked about it on the ship. For some strange reason, China seemed a likely place.

When we got into bed and turned off the light, the weirdest thing happened. At first I couldn't believe it. But I was there.

The room was black and then a faint blood red glow began seeping from beneath the heavy felt curtains. I was too terrified to make a sound. Something was definitely lurking in the shadows.

"There's something evil in here," Nanci sat bolt upright and shouted. "Start praying, quick!"

Instead, I started gagging. A foul smell filled the room. My chest felt like someone was sitting on it. I had to get out of there. I'd heard of encounters with demonic forces, certainly, but it had never happened to me.

I reached out, and my hand fell on my Bible, which I kept beside me when I slept. I clutched it to my chest. Groping above my head, I pulled a little chain to turn on the bed light. The ruddy glow dimmed, but remained.

I knew instinctively what to do. We began our counter-attack. Most of the night, we took turns reading aloud from the Bible, praying, and singing. I set my tiny cassette player next to us, and a steady stream of praise music poured out. We discussed the story of Joshua and his men marching around Jericho, claiming the land for God.

I suggested we do the same. We climbed out of bed—by this time we were in the same bed—and, feeling a bit silly at first, marched around the perimeter of the room in our nightgowns. Walking over the beds, behind the curtains, around the chairs, and into the bathroom, we claimed our little territory for God with each step.

After awhile, the glow began to pale and the smell subsided. We knew that we had fought a mighty battle. And we had won.

As I turned off the light, Nanci had one more comment. "We're okay now, but I have a feeling like I've never had before. I feel like we might not get out of China alive."

———————————

Hundreds of Chinese lined the sidewalks each morning to practice *Tai Chi*—a slow, rhythmic exercise. The older ones wore pajama-like Mao suits—men in navy blue, women in muted floral prints. The less traditional younger ones performed the ancient rituals to the sound of twangy Chinese tunes blaring from Western "ghetto blasters."

Bicycles jammed the streets. People strolled around holding pet birds in cages; occasionally a woman rode by with a live duck in the basket of her bike. Chickens were carried upside down with their feet bound together.

We decided the best place to meet the Chinese was on their turf, so we rented bikes every morning. We stopped at parks, monuments, restaurants, and shops, hoping to strike up a conversation.

The crowded markets held great promise for prospects. Guangzhou was known for its open-air markets, where everything from bear claws (not the pastries) to kittens to snakes, all for human consumption, was sold. We looked for fresh fruit and vegetables. The fruit stands always seemed to be behind the meat sections, directly behind the snake salesmen, in fact.

As I approached one fruit stand, I saw a man disentangle a live water snake from a large tub full of them. He killed it by stabbing it in the head, then pinned the head to a long board and sliced it down the middle to extricate the meat. Blood ran everywhere. I hurried away, having lost my appetite.

We met people who seemed eager to speak to us. Just when I felt encouraged, the old familiar question cropped up: "Change money?" They feigned interest in what we were saying so that they could ask for our FEC money.

One afternoon, as we stood watching swans glide across a lake in a park, someone tapped my shoulder. I turned to find a bony, young Chinese man. He motioned with his eyes to an artifact he held carefully in his hand.

Looking over his shoulder, he removed the lid from a small metal container. I peered inside at some fine white powder. I remembered that the penalty for drug possession was a firing squad, and quickly pushed him away.

I wrote in my journal that night: "Still nothing to report."

We debated returning to Hong Kong, and begged for God to give us a sign if He wanted us to stay in China.

Wandering aimlessly through the alleyways, I caught a glimpse of Jesus' face through a doorway we passed. I called out to Nanci, who'd moved on ahead, and motioned her back. We carefully peered into the room, and there on the wall was a poster of Jesus. A hunched old woman appeared and startled us. Through hand gestures, we told her that we were Christians, and asked if she was, too.

She pointed to the picture and then to her heart, embracing herself and gazing upward. We did the same. We knew now that we would stay the full time.

Hours later, we returned to the woman's house. This time, I had a Bible bookmark and a Chinese New Testament concealed in my backpack. When we knocked, she motioned us inside, and I handed her the bookmark. Because of the possible danger to her, I wasn't sure whether or not to give her the New Testament. So I prayed for a sign. My prayer was immediately answered. A large, imposing woman appeared and filled the doorway. The old lady was visibly shaken, and slipped the bookmark into her pocket. So this was how the neighborhood watch worked! We bowed to the old lady and left, thankful that the other woman apparently didn't recognize the face on the poster.

We headed north on a grueling two-and-a-half day barge and bus ride. Our first leg of the trip was a 21-1/2 hour ride up the Pearl River on a three-level floating dorm. Two shelves extended about six feet from the wall around the perimeter of each level. They served as community bunk beds, with a two-inch board separating each space. Hundreds of people packed into each level. Those who couldn't afford a place on the platform beds slept in lounge chairs.

Bells rang to signal mealtimes, and men appeared with bowls of soup, rice, and vegetables. They scurried around selling their wares, then disappeared to some unseen kitchen until time to eat again. The heat and noise were a constant annoyance. We observed that contrary to our previous ideas about Asians, the Chinese were neither shy nor reticent.

No matter where he is, every Chinese man starts his day by exercising his throat muscles through loud throat-clearing and spitting. We had become accustomed to this early morning ritual, so it was no surprise when spitting began at daybreak. For the equivalent of a four-dollar ticket, who could complain?

We spent the night in an industrial city before continuing our journey. At 6:30 a.m., I ran to the bathroom. I was a victim of "the chopstick canter." For the next two hours, my body was in total, violent revolt. My fever shot up. Nanci left to get us another room, because both our toilet and our air conditioner had quit working at the same time.

"I'm going to die here in this awful city," I cried, recalling Nanci's warning that we might not get out of China alive. I lay there waiting for my demise.

The door creaked open and a maid entered. Seeing me sprawled on the floor, she mopped around me, picked up the dirty towels, plumped the bed, and left.

Then, as quickly as it had come upon me, my mysterious illness left. When Nanci returned, her freckled face crinkled with worry, I was sitting up in bed, smiling. I was even hungry.

———————

The next portion of our journey was a ten-hour bus ride to Guilin. Ours were the only white faces aboard. Our bus resembled the abandoned ones seen along the roadside in the United States.

We handed the conductor our tickets, which even had seat assignments stamped on them. *Seat* was a misnomer: this bus had benches.

The woman next to me held a baby boy on her lap. A few minutes into the ride, she lowered his pants and held him up in the air so that he urinated toward the woman's head in front of us. He narrowly missed her, but he did manage to wet the inside of her open bag and a number of objects in the aisle. Unbelievable shouting broke out. Oh, how we wished we understood Chinese!

The next time the boy needed to relieve himself, his mother passed her son to the man sitting next to the window, and motioned for him to hold the baby out the window. It was anyone's guess who was more terrified—the baby or the passengers sitting downwind.

We arrived in Guilin with high hopes. The smaller towns and villages gave us a truer picture of China. The vast majority of Chinese live outside the country's few metropolises, and work as simple farmers or proprietors of roadside stands. The closest thing they have to convenience stores are olive green refrigerators sitting by the side of the road. For the equivalent of a quarter, you can buy a soft drink, but it must be consumed on the spot so the proprietor can keep the container.

We were to be in Guilin for Moon Day, a major festival which occurs on the 15th day of the eighth moon (Chinese calendar), when the moon is at its brightest. It's a time when families gather to celebrate the harvest, pay homage to ancestors, and exchange moon cakes, little square pastries filled with sweet mung bean.

We joined the promenade along the riverfront, stopping from time to time to point at the full moon as everyone else was doing. Men played cards in little shacks by the light of kerosene lamps. Women sat on the ground, either knitting or washing their dishes in the street. We passed an old woman sitting alone on a tiny footstool. I couldn't get her face out of my mind.

When we came upon a roadside stand selling moon cakes, I stopped. "I need to get something," I said to Nanci.

I bought one and headed back to the old woman. Bending down, I held out the carefully wrapped cake. She stared at it, then at me. Smiling, she took it, and motioned for us to sit on the dirt. We tried our few Chinese words, but conversation was impossible. When we rose to leave, Nanci pressed a little jade cross into the woman's hand. We hoped she understood our message.

Yang-chou was our last hope of witnessing in China. Like in Guilin, we quickly found a favorite restaurant. Susanna, the proprietor, spoke flawless English and specialized in peanut butter banana pancakes.

When business was slow, we sat with her for hours to discuss her life and work, always waiting for a chance to share our faith. It never came. Something told us that as friendly as she was, it would be dangerous to bring up the subject.

So we packed to leave China, feeling defeated. We had had few opportunities and no concrete victories. As we closed our bags, Nanci seemed unusually pensive.

"What are you thinking?" I asked.

"As I was praying last night, I had a vision of a garden planted for harvest, but nothing was showing yet. A man tended it diligently. Still nothing grew. Yet he knew that someday it would blossom.

"I think it was a message from God. We're not to see the fruits of our work. That's His business. We're just to be faithful gardeners."

I thought about the old woman in Guangzhou with the Jesus picture in her home. Then a man we'd met in a park who'd gone to prison for his Christian beliefs. Two college students at the state-run TSM Church (Three Self Movement) had become Christians through a missionary teaching English. Something was growing in China.

Now I understood the ancient Chinese proverb that a young man told us when we first entered the country.

"The moon is not round in China," he said. "Even though it looks the same as in the rest of the world, it isn't. Life here is never as it appears on the surface."

Leaving to return to Hong Kong, I reflected on our time in China. We had learned what it was like to do spiritual battle in a hard place where there isn't always a happy ending. I also remembered Nanci's dire prediction at the beginning of our stay. It was true—a part of us had died in China: our expectations.

6

Reaching Out (Stacy)

As soon as we got back to Hong Kong, we headed straight to the YWAM headquarters located in a converted hospital overlooking the harbor. Over 60 missionaries were being housed there, so we were delighted when they said they had room for us. They assigned us to the "upper *amah*" section, which sounded quaint. Then I remembered that *amah* meant "maid."

Our room was in a small building separate from the rest of the base. We were a little discouraged when our bathroom was pointed out—down a flight of stairs, across a parking lot, and up two more flights of stairs.

Once settled, we rushed off to make arrangements to visit the main thing we wanted to see: the Walled City.

There's a seldom-seen side of Hong Kong where Triad (Chinese Mafia) gangs rule, defying the neat, tidy legal system set up by the law-abiding British. The gangs control the drug traffic, prostitution, and most other forms of vice. We were about to invade their territory.

The Walled City is a section of the downtown area where thousands live densely packed into haphazardly constructed buildings. We joined eight volunteers who were regular members of a Wednesday night group which worked at "The Well." A small Chinese man motioned for us to follow him into the tight underground passageways that thread the maze.

I turned sideways, squeezed through a crack in the wall, stepped down into a dark corridor, and ducked to avoid electrical wires hanging overhead.

"Be careful of the wires," he yelled. "It's electricity stolen from outside. Watch your step, too; there's no sewer system down here."

We passed alcoves where people had made a home or shop. Their expressionless eyes followed as we hurried by. I dodged water dripping from the overhead wires, and fell to the back of the group to explore. Just as I turned on my camera's flash, something rustled nearby. I jumped, and looked down to see an old woman chuckling at me. Sorting through a garbage heap, she pointed to the ground where a family of rats raced her for something to eat.

As we rounded a corner, we saw a sign that read "The Well" over the door into a well-lit room. Soft music was playing, and fifty to sixty people were already there.

It was to this place that British-born Jackie Pullinger had ventured alone 20 years ago to begin a ministry to drug addicts and gang members. Today, her work is world renowned, and she and her staff boast the most successful drug rehabilitation program in all of Hong Kong. We were here for their weekly Bible study.

As first-timers, Nanci and I were pulled aside for an explanation of what would take place. The rest of our group went about their assigned duties.

"Men and women will drift in over the next few hours. We ask you to talk and pray with any who speak English then we'll have a worship service," a volunteer told us.

"This is the first step many people take to get their lives in order. If someone seems serious about breaking his heroin addiction, let me know. We have a number of detox centers on the outer islands where staff members will pray with them around the clock, and teach them how to pray for themselves. They detoxify without any withdrawal symptoms, using prayer as their only medicine."

He must have seen the skepticism in my eyes.

"I know it sounds strange, but I was one of them. So

were most of the other volunteers here. When we felt strong enough to return to normal life, we were taken to Hang Fook Camp in Kowloon, where we lived in a compound with hundreds of other people in our same situation, learning job skills."

By now, stragglers had begun filtering in, depositing their shoes at the door and milling about. Nanci and I joined forces with a staff member until we felt bold enough to go solo. During the two-hour service that evening, three men came forward to seek help.

Two nights later, we met Samuel Lai, a former resident of the Walled City. Samuel had started a church near Temple Street. We arranged to go with him and others on a street mission.

On the third floor of an empty office building, we walked down a hall until we came to a sign that read "Wanchai Church." The room was empty, but the door was unlocked, so we entered and waited.

Soon, a group of Chinese people entered, led by Samuel and an American missionary. After song and prayer, the evening's program was announced: who would deliver the message, which drama would be performed, and which songs would be sung. As we left the room, we were handed bundles of tracts to hand out.

I was not particularly looking forward to this. I never knew what to say or do when street witnessing. I slipped the bundles into my daypack, and decided I'd dispose of them later.

"I think you'll enjoy tonight," Samuel said as we headed toward Temple Street. "One never knows what will happen there."

Temple Street is a popular tourist spot because of its rich night life. In the evening, it takes on the air of a carnival, with prostitutes and drug dealers working alongside fortune-telling booths and palm readers. Elaborate

Chinese dramas are enacted on the street.

"Most of the people in our church came right off this street," Samuel said. "My first night of outreach here, over a year ago, I witnessed a real miracle. A man who was blind in one eye came forward for prayer. We prayed for him, and his eye was healed. Word spread quickly. People began saying that our God was more powerful than theirs."

We staked a place on the sidewalk between a fortune teller and a drama group. Using a portable speaker, Samuel led some spirited worship songs. A large crowd gathered. Testimonies and a religious drama were presented. People stayed, and they paid rapt attention.

I pulled a few tracts from my daypack and quietly held them up. The man next to me grabbed one. Others followed. I pulled more from my bag, and they were quickly gone. Nanci was having the same experience. Soon I was stopping passersby and offering them tracts.

"Nanci, Stacy, can you come here?" Samuel pleaded.

He pointed to two "seers" who were loudly telling the crowd not to listen. They were upset because their business suffered when people became interested in the Christian God.

Samuel asked us to be decoys. So we conversed with the "seers" through hand gestures for almost an hour to prevent Samuel's work from being disrupted. Even our limited abilities were useful that night.

A few nights later, we experienced a different type of outreach. Each Friday, a group gathered at the Star Ferry and split into teams to feed the "street sleepers." I had participated in many food programs before, but they always took place in church halls or shelters.

When our team reached its assigned area, the odor of rotten food and garbage assaulted our noses. Smelly litter lined the sidewalks and gutters. The odor of urine, unwashed bodies, and filthy clothing was unmistakable.

Overwhelming heat and humidity only intensified the misery. By some unspoken agreement, we all willed ourselves not to take notice, or at least not to comment on the horrible conditions.

I was astounded at how many places people could find to bed down. Along the street they were crouched in entry ways, alcoves, and under stairways. Many were lying on beds of rags or discarded boxes. Large pieces of cardboard leaned against the cold stone walls or were propped against each other to form some semblance of privacy. Paper sacks held the people's personal belongings. Though the street people moved about from week to week, their faces seldom changed.

Our team brought in box dinners, clothes, and blankets. They also brought limited medical supplies to treat minor injuries. The volunteers expected nothing in return, which was just as well, because few of the people even acknowledged their presence.

The first "regular" we encountered cowered in a dark cavity up a few steps from street level, almost completely obscured by cardboard. He smelled of cheap wine and his beard and moustache were speckled with crumbs.

We learned that for over a year the team had cared for this particular man. One of the men on the team handed him a box of food and a clean change of clothes and then matter-of-factly began treating his infected eye.

"Your eye looks better," he said. "Are you ready for a bath?"

"Not this week. Maybe next time."

We gathered in a circle around the fragile man, clasped hands, and prayed. Then we moved on.

———————

Hong Kong lived up to all that we expected of it; we found the energy and diversity of the area riveting. In contrast to China, the Chinese people here openly practiced ancestral worship. Breadbox-sized "god houses," in reality altars for small idols, were nailed to the front of homes and shops. Red lights illuminated them and joss sticks burned constantly in front of them. A heady perfume of incense seemed to ascend heavenward at all times.

While we were in Hong Kong, we regularly attended a church at the bottom of the hill below the YWAM headquarters. Its congregation consisted mostly of Filipino *amahs*. Ironically, we realized that we had come to identify much more with these humble souls than we had with the cosmopolitan crowd of the tourist districts. Somewhere along the way, we had painlessly slipped into the role of servant.

7

Making Friends with Rice (Stacy)

The bus dropped us off at a taxi stand in Jakarta on a sweltering Sunday afternoon. There were no taxis, only groups of leering men who pressed their faces close to mine and pulled at my clothes until I yelled out to Nanci in panic.

A muffled "Over here!" came back, and I laughed with relief when I saw Nanci's head bobbing up and down. Thank goodness she was so tall.

Using shoulders and bags to clear a path, I tossed a disgusted look over my shoulder at the men. I was not impressed with my first experience in a Muslim country.

The Jakarta base director had invited us to spend a month in Indonesia, and we had sent letters and telegrams announcing our arrival time. But we never received a reply, and no one was waiting to meet us when we arrived. Indonesian mail service was "hit-or-miss," so we had no idea if we were expected or not.

On our bus ride into town, we saw patches of green rice paddies framed with banana trees and towering palms. Wearing coolie hats that looked like inverted bamboo baskets, men and women painstakingly planted seedlings by hand. Older men guided water buffalo through the marshy fields.

I was surprised at the appearance of the people. They looked more Indian than I expected, with high cheekbones and round eyes. The women were more robust than their other Asian counterparts. When an Indonesian grinned, dazzling white teeth contrasted strongly with brown skin.

The more affluent homes had orange tiled roofs and dark brick sides, a relic of the colonial Dutch influence. Clustered around these homes were tiny bamboo shacks housing the poorer class. Children swam in canals in the middle of the road, but these canals were actually open sewers which carried refuse out to sea.

At the airport, we had tried one last time to reach YWAM by phone, with no results. So we opted to spend the night at a guest house listed in our *Shoestring Guide to Southeast Asia*. The desk clerk looked askance over the top of his glasses when we told him that we were traveling alone. But his business sense overruled his moral indignation, and he handed us a key. The guide book had described our lodge as "pretty plain, but fair value....Clean and friendly, with a pleasant balcony at the back."

The "plain" was accurate. Our 6-by-8-foot room contained two simple cots and a decrepit fan. Floor, walls, and ceiling were cement. It had to be easy to clean, because it could be hosed down. "Fair value" was also correct; where else could you get two beds and breakfast in a major downtown setting for $2.50 per person?

By daylight, even a cold shower sounded good. A good part of the day was spent trying to find the YWAM base; missionaries don't exactly advertise in Indonesia. We made phone calls all morning. We finally made contact, and a young woman invited us to "come on over." At least, that's what I thought she said. Her English was so limited that all I could make out was: "turn left at the store, right at the green fence, left at the black gate."

We hailed a Blue Bird (the best taxis in Indonesia) and directed the driver to the extreme southern part of Jakarta. An hour later, we were circling the same six blocks. Finally, the driver flagged down some children and

asked for help. They eagerly nodded that they knew where
we wanted to go, so we followed slowly behind their bikes
as they pedaled furiously down the center of the road.
Unfortunately, their knowledge didn't match their enthusiasm, and we were circling the same blocks once again.

Part of the problem was that our driver spoke no English. I tried to explain directions with the aid of an
Indonesian phrase book, only to discover that he spoke no
Indonesian either! This was my first indication of the
enormous ethnic and linguistic diversity of the country.

Two hours and many dirt roads later, Nanci peered over
the gate to a place that fit the description we had been
given. When she turned around, her smile told me that we
had found it.

The Jakarta base was on the grounds of a large estate
loaned indefinitely to YWAM by a Christian businessman.
It was home, office, and school for 12 Indonesian workers
and their guests.

Among the guests was a team of 16 from Finland,
studying for four months at the School of Evangelism
(SOE). There was also a Catholic priest/globe-trotting
missionary in his 60s who kept everyone enthralled with
his stories of hitchhiking the entire length of Japan.

Meals were the highlight of each day. Ibu Phony, with
a background as a caterer, presided over the kitchen. *Ibu*
was a term of endearment meaning "mother." She always
prepared more than enough food, and made certain that
everyone took seconds.

"I'm gonna fatten you girls up," Ibu said, leading us to
a table with trays of tempting delicacies arranged around
a large floral centerpiece. It looked more like a wedding
buffet than a meal at a mission base.

"Have some *nasi goreng* [fried rice]," she urged. "Take
more *satay* [tiny kebabs]," she insisted, piling the skew-
ered chicken and creamy peanut sauce on my plate. She
guided me toward a spicy shrimp dish, a plate of hard-

boiled eggs in pastry batter, and a bowl of succulent fruits and vegetables. There were even two Finnish dishes in honor of the Finns.

"That's not enough rice," she scolded, heaping another mound onto my plate. "In Indonesia, we say that an Indonesian hasn't eaten until he's eaten his rice."

It was clear that if we wanted to be accepted into this culture, we were going to have to eat a lot of rice.

The director of the School of Evangelism invited us to join the group, which had just begun, and complete the entire four months of training. When we told him that we lacked the time, he said we were welcome to attend the next eight days of lectures on the government, culture, religion, and Christian revival taking place in Indonesia.

Our professor was Herman Weitts, an endearing Dutch-American in his mid-40s, who held several advanced degrees and spoke ten languages. Herman was newly married to a beautiful Indonesian woman.

Five years earlier, Herman was attending a YWAM Leadership Training School in Kona, Hawaii. He had been earnestly praying for God's direction in his life. A voice awakened him in the middle of the night, and told him to establish an orphanage on the tiny island of Nias.

At dawn, Herman rushed to find an atlas and see where Nias was located. Upon learning that it was an Indonesian island, he rejoiced because of his familiarity with the country from previous mission trips and his Dutch heritage. He began attending language classes, where he met the schoolteacher who was to become his wife. Herman and his wife were the first of many special friends God was to bring into our lives.

Indonesia covers an expanse as vast as the distance from California to Bermuda, and is made up of 13,677 islands. It is the most populous Muslim country in the world, and Jakarta is the world's largest Muslim city. The Islam of Indonesia is quite different from its counterparts elsewhere. It has much more to do with cultural rules and festivals than with religious beliefs, and lacks the extreme fanaticism found in the Arab world.

Every adult is required to register with the government his membership in one of five state-approved religions: Islam, Buddhism, Hinduism, Christianity, or animism. Islam claims the largest following by far, approximately 83 percent of the population.

Religious registration is actually more a political necessity than a statement of faith. In 1965, a failed coup was led by a Communist insurgency group. To prevent a similar occurrence, this law was enacted on the assumption that since Communists are avowed atheists, refusal to register religion was tantamount to admission of Communist leanings.

Indonesia is the only Muslim country in the world where significant numbers of Muslims are turning to the Lord. The revival began in the early 1900s, and has been exploding since 1964. From 1980 to 1985, 1.5 million Muslims embraced Christianity, proof that Indonesians have been encountering God in powerful personal ways.

But no matter what they call themselves, most still pay homage to animistic tribal gods. Witchcraft, sorcery, and black magic are an integral part of their lives.

For instance, a unique type of auto body shop thrives in Jakarta. It is attended by a witch doctor who places a special cover over the car, recites incantations to evoke healing gods, and then lifts the cover to reveal a totally "repaired" car. To the Western mind this sounds ludicrous; to the Indonesian, it's cheaper and certainly faster!

Some of the most important information Herman passed on to us involved the Indonesian culture:

- The feet are seen as the lowliest part of the body.
- It is a serious insult to sit in such a way that the soles of the feet face someone.

- It is impolite to use the toes for pointing.

- Aggressive gestures and postures such as crossing arms over the chest or standing with hands on the hips are regarded as bad manners.

- Loud voices are particularly offensive.

- The more important and vehement the subject under discussion, the quieter the voice becomes.

- To beckon with a crooked finger is rude.

- The thumb rather than the forefinger should be used for pointing.

- Nothing should be given or received with the left hand.

- A nose is never blown in public.

- Never eat until told to begin, and always wait until invited to take seconds.

We were horrified to realize how many of these social rules we had already broken in just one week in the country. We were also told that we were a curiosity because we were unmarried at our age.

When not in class, we hired a *becak* (pronounced bay-chak) to go exploring. A *becak* is a bicycle-powered taxi. A bench seat long enough for three people rests on two large wheels on the front. A hood provides shelter from the sun. Behind it, the driver perches high above a larger wheel, which enables him to see how to steer.

At first, I felt like the "ugly American" riding in these, but I quickly became accustomed to them, since they were the major form of transportation for short distances. My heart always raced when we pulled into traffic alongside fast-moving cars, trucks, motorcycles, and lumbering ox-drawn carts.

Johnny and Melci, an Indonesian couple at the School

of Evangelism, became our instant friends. Johnny was a slender young man with riveting eyes and boundless energy. Before he came to the school, Johnny and another Indonesian missionary had led a discipleship group of more than 100 new, young Christians. His ambition was to return to his home island of Timor and lead teams into the remote regions. His playful wife Melci was a perfect complement with her hospitality and administration.

Johnny worked as a tailor whenever he needed money for himself, his wife, and their three-year-old daughter Stephanie. To earn extra income, Melci sold batik dresses handmade by a friend. They were dedicated students and tireless workers.

Little Stephanie was a bundle of energy. Her large Oreo-cookie eyes twinkled whenever she spoke, and her hair clustered in curls around her head. She skipped about the grounds, singing praise songs and carrying on private conversations with Jesus.

"I wanted a watch real bad," Stephanie told me one day. "I asked my parents for one, but they said they didn't have enough money. So I just asked God."

Weeks later, a visitor, completely unaware of her prayers, surprised her with a gift: a watch. When I asked to see it, she replied, "My daddy is borrowing it. He borrows it a lot. I told him he should ask God for one, too." I whispered to Stephanie to ask God if he could find a suitable mate for Nanci and me.

8

My Island Paradise (Stacy)

After our time in Jakarta, we headed for the island of Bali. We arrived at the Yogyakarta station in plenty of time to find a bus to take us to the ferry for Denpasar, Bali's capital. Unlike the United States, where a few major companies have cornered the bus market, Indonesia has many private companies, with differing degrees of service. We had no idea which to choose, so we chose a company which promised 17 hours of air-conditioned comfort as well as dinner, breakfast, and a ferry ride—all for eight dollars.

I was thrilled that our bus looked so modern. It even had indoor plumbing. The seats were plush blue velvet recliners spaced well apart. My excitement grew with each mile. I was on my way to Bali, my dream destination ever since I had seen the movie *South Pacific*. I could almost see Rossano Brazzi waiting for me on the beach.

Suddenly, the air conditioning stopped. It wasn't just a brief shutdown; there was a definite finality to its cessation. Passengers began wildly fanning themselves. Our two Indonesian attendants pulled out some tools and went to work on the device. Their mechanical abilities were evidently nil, because it was soon announced that we would stop at a mechanic's house in the next town—"the best mechanic in all of Indonesia."

We reached Surakarta, and wove through a labyrinth of back streets to a small shack. A little old man rushed out, tool kit in hand. Within ten minutes, the blown fuse was replaced and we were on our way.

Twenty minutes later, the air conditioner cut off again, so we stopped for dinner. Dinner was served on a dirt parking lot. We were given sodas and bowls of something that turned out to be rice with assorted toppings. Some people (like Nanci) got nice things like fried eggs, chicken, or vegetables. I got a grayish, rubbery substance. Nanci was kind enough to share hers with me, and with enough hot sauce, it was palatable.

In the meantime, the driver worked on the air conditioner. When we piled back on, it was already cool, and I thanked him profusely. I reasoned that a little positive reinforcement might encourage him to continue striving to please. A few minutes later, the system shut down again. At this point, even I gave up. The windows were the type that could not be opened. The more I thought about it, the more claustrophobic I became. Nanci's strategy was to pour herself into a book and get her mind off the situation. For a few minutes, I hated her.

When I could stand it no longer, I stomped up and down the aisle and glowered at everyone. At the back of the bus, I discovered a tiny vent above the stacks of boxes and excess luggage. Luckily, since I was so short, I was able to stand on a box and hold my head so that a small bit of air blew across my face from time to time. It wasn't much, and it wasn't cool, but at least it was fresh air. I stood there hour after hour, pressing my nose into the vent. Some of the passengers occasionally turned to stare at me. All except Nanci. She just kept reading. I hated her.

When breakfast was served at 3:00 a.m., I returned to my seat. Dim lights flickered on, and little white boxes were passed out. I cautiously opened mine, hoping my luck had improved since dinner. It had a hard-boiled egg, toast, and something purple, which I assumed was fruit.

As I started to take a bite, a cockroach crawled out from underneath my bread and plopped onto my lap.

Nanci shared her breakfast with me.

When our bus stopped, I stood and looked out the window. We were surrounded by other buses, all filled with passengers waiting in air-conditioned comfort. Out of the blackness, I saw something large with flashing red lights, and it was headed straight for us. It was the ferry that was going to deliver us to Bali, my South Pacific paradise.

————————————

Denpasar was a monument to noise, pollution, and every form of hustling. Our arrival was again unexpected, in spite of copious correspondence. However, Yayasan Wahana Anak Muda (YWAM-Bali) graciously made room.

On our first afternoon, we walked to Kuta Beach, described in our tour book as "the armpit and sleaze bomb" of Bali. Tourists were out in their usual raucous form; buses shuttled contestants between bars in city-sponsored drinking contests. Toplessness was the norm for the natives; nudity was supposedly permitted, although we never saw any.

Enterprising Balinese sold everything from massages to hairdos on the beach; plaiting hair was big business. The only thing you couldn't buy was privacy.

In addition to the Western influence that had blatantly invaded the island, we had a unique opportunity to observe a bit of Bali's culture at the beach. We weren't sure what kind of ceremony we had wandered upon. Women in lavish floral sarongs danced before a group of older men, probably village seers. The women wore extravagant necklaces and bundles of bracelets that clicked and clanged as they swayed to the constant beating of drums. We were later told that drums were used both to provide a musical cadence and to invite the gods to come join the festivities.

Activity was centered around a high platform on top of bamboo poles. It was decorated with fresh flowers, white cloth, and colored paper. Chanting and the passing of a communal cup were part of the ceremony.

The next day, we learned more about Balinese rituals and customs while interviewing Joel, the YWAM base director. Whether working or playing, the Balinese approach life with theatrical flair. Their life centers around religion from birth until death, and they live in constant fear of their gods.

The Hindus of Indonesia fled to Bali when the Muslims took over in the 1400s. Bali is the largest Hindu outpost in the world outside of India. The Balinese brand of Hinduism is far different from that practiced in India. It's very involved with black magic and the occult.

Balinese Hindus observe more than 60 religious holidays each year. The basic tenet of their religion is the belief that the island is owned by the supreme god Sanghyang Widhi, and has been handed down to the people in sacred trust. In return, the people show their gratitude by filling their lives with symbolic activities and worship, devoting most of their waking hours to an endless series of offerings, purifications, temple festivities, processions, dances, cremations, and dozens of other religious rites. Thousands of temples adorn the island.

I remembered stepping over hundreds of little 4-by-4-inch square baskets handmade from wide banana leaves when we first arrived. They were known as *ngedjot,* and contained assorted gifts for the gods, like grains of rice, flowers, salt, or a pinch of chili pepper. They are placed in front of homes or offices to ensure protection and prosperity for occupants. Some are put on high shelves for the "good" gods and some on the ground for the "baddies." No one dares engage in any activity until the *ngedjot* are safely out each morning. However, as soon as they are set down, the infamous Balinese dogs begin nosing them in hopes of finding food. It was hard to understand why this wasn't considered a desecration.

According to our handbook on Indonesia, the Balinese are "scared witless of ghosts and goblins, which disguise themselves as black cats, naked women, and crows." Their gods and goddesses sometimes inhabit stone statues or fly through the air while deciding whether to protect or harm someone. From time to time, the Balinese invite different gods to earth, feed and entertain them, then send them back home because they're too expensive to maintain.

One afternoon, we met a Balinese man who had recently become a Christian. He told us about all the statues that abound in Bali, stone figures representing gods. They are clothed in brightly colored dresses, some with umbrellas over their heads to shade them from the sun. Food is offered to them daily. Occasionally, the smaller, portable ones are taken to the beach and bathed. In essence, they are treated like living people.

When asked what it was like to become a Christian, he responded, "It's great to finally have a God who will take care of me."

———————

Joel's description of life in Bali explained why such a dark cloud seemed to hang over the island. Although there were a few Christians, years of missionary work had yielded little fruit.

Joel cautioned us to be careful walking around the city. "Men who possess spiritual powers often go down to the tourist area and tease Western women," he said.

"They may try to touch you. You can recognize them by the evil, empty look in their eyes. When they place their hands on you, they are transferring a spell conjured up by their black magic. Stay away from them," he warned.

My idyllic image of an island paradise was crumbling. How could any Hindu convert to Christianity with such a legacy? Sharing Christ with the tourists seemed a more hopeful prospect.

Joel read our thoughts. "The best way to reach the Balinese for Christ is through miracles," he said. Again, we needed the overwhelming display of God's power.

"For a Balinese Hindu to become a Christian means going against centuries of tradition," he said. "It's too scary. Inheritances are cut off; individuals are cast out of their villages. Their friends and family turn against them."

The YWAM work in Bali began in May of 1986 with Joel, his wife, and a handful of volunteers. Today, close to 20 workers put in long, frustrating hours without seeing many results. Most of their work is concentrated in orphanages and prisons. They have also started churches in small villages such as Ubud, a beautiful, artsy community in the cool hills 40 minutes from the beach.

Ubud is a center for Balinese art and religion, but it's also a haven for the New Age movement. Thousands of foreigners visit each year, searching for nirvana within themselves while embracing Balinese Hinduism. Some never return home, choosing to remain and hang out in restaurants which feature oversized floor pillows, herbal tea, and chains of beads. They spend their days talking among themselves and listening to Eastern music.

We stayed in Ubud for a week, living with an American missionary couple who had spent almost 35 years in Bali. Everyone in town knew Roger and Leila Lewis and respected them. A good part of their time was spent ministering to New Agers who'd become disillusioned with their beliefs or had totally lost touch with reality.

We learned something about the work of church planting. The Lewises kept in constant contact with communities where they had founded churches. There were Bible studies to be prepared and church services to be planned. There were home visits and counseling sessions, and always a steady stream of visitors, phone calls, and crises.

Sunday morning, in the midst of a tropical rainstorm, we joined the Lewises in the first church ever established in Ubud. The service was simple and traditional. Leila played hymns on her portable battery-operated keyboard. Then there were prayers and testimonies. The service was nothing special, unless you considered the obstacles against ever starting a church in this community.

Afterward, rain still pouring, we walked with a group to the home of a paraplegic. We conducted a private service for this lone young Christian living with a Hindu family, repeating the one given earlier.

Bali was one of the places on our trip which only time and distance let me remember with any fondness. We were exhausted by the time we left Bali to head to Thailand, but the zeal of the Balinese workers would long be remembered. Though the island failed to live up to my expectations, I felt I had glimpsed paradise through these faithful workers.

9

No-Man's-Land (Nanci)

"Twenty-five baht," I insisted. "No more."

"Thirty," he repeated, and folded his arms.

Stacy and I climbed aboard the *tuk-tuk* and handed 30 baht to the driver. *Tuk-tuks* are brightly painted tin carts propelled by noisy motorcycle engines. Since they are barely large enough for three thin passengers, two people with luggage are a tight squeeze. Cheaper than taxis and more convenient than buses, *tuk-tuks* are the backbone of public transportation in Thailand.

"Why didn't you hold out?" Stacy growled.

"Because we're late," I snapped back. I was impatient with negotiating the price for everything.

We were catching a bus for Aranyaprathet. This small town on the Thai-Cambodian border was a hub for relief organizations working in the refugee camps. The camps housed Vietnamese, Cambodians, and Laotians who had fled when Communists came into power in the mid-1970s.

This was the one place I had insisted we include in our itinerary. Years earlier, I'd attended a going-away party for a friend whose job had involved resettling Southeast Asian refugees. I sat spellbound, listening to a Cambodian family tell of narrowly escaping their homeland only to endure extreme hardships in a camp in Thailand. They had every reason to be bitter, but instead, they were busy forging a new life and helping other expatriates get established.

After that night, I read everything I could find about the refugee situation. The more I learned, the more determined I became to work in one of the Thai camps.

When we arrived in Aranyaprathet, we waved aside the usual eager offers of assistance, more often motivated by economics than by human kindness. We hoisted our bags and took off along a dusty road flanked by palm trees and flooded rice paddies. We recognized the mission house by the large number of bicycles out front. Team members all used old-fashioned one-speed bicycles to commute to town for supplies and for travel between team houses.

One of the team members directed us to a room in the main house, which was used for meetings and meals. The house had a sharply slanting roof, which the Thais believe prevent evil spirits from resting on the house.

After we got settled, we went back to the living room. A young, slender blonde with a New Zealand accent greeted us, quickly dispensing with all formalities.

"You must be Stacy and Nanci. I'm Elaine. Come in and have a 'cuppa.'" It was a relief to be expected somewhere. Over tea and scones, the team leader explained the work of the volunteers.

"We have several teams working in the refugee camp. One runs a preschool; others run the post office and the bank. Before those were set up, mail with checks was constantly pilfered. Refugees are an easy target, because they have no rights in Thai society."

I got right to the point. "When can we go to the camps?" I asked.

"We'll see," she hesitated. "I'm still trying to get clearance for you. We only get a few guest passes each year, because the government has been embarrassed by all the negative reports in the international press. They've threatened to quit giving out passes entirely."

I suppressed a frown. I'd traveled halfway around the world. I'd never thought that I'd have trouble getting in.

"There's a BBC documentary on the refugee situation you might like. I'll have someone set up the VCR for you."

We were totally unprepared for the horrors we saw.

One scene showed a glass case, extending from floor to ceiling along an entire wall, holding hundreds of sun-bleached skulls. "This is a museum in Phnom Penh, the capital of Cambodia," the narrator said. "The government has preserved these skulls as a reminder of the atrocities committed under Pol Pot. During his regime from 1975 to 1979, over one million Cambodians were executed. Their only crime was that they wore glasses or spoke a foreign language—a sign that they were intellectuals, avowed enemies of the peasant-dominated government.

"Those who weren't killed were forced to work 12 to 15 hours a day in rice fields. If they faltered, they were brutally beaten. Their supervisors were uneducated peasants, barely teenagers."

The documentary flashed to a wooden fishing boat filled with almost-naked bodies huddled together against the rain. The camera zoomed in on faces which reflected no emotion, not even fear. Even the children's faces were expressionless.

The narrator continued, "When the Communists came into power, thousands of Vietnamese spent their life savings for passage on boats like this or even on non-existent boats. If the boats didn't sink, they were often seized by pirates, who stole what little the refugees had been able to sneak out. Even if the refugees survived the harrowing journey to a safe country, they risked being turned back on arrival. The lucky ones were put in camps. Many are still there after ten years, waiting for permission to leave."

The camera toured a typical camp in Thailand: buildings made of bamboo and thatch, sealed off from the outside world by imposing tangles of barbed wire. I wondered if this would be my closest look at a camp.

At breakfast the next morning, I listened with envy as everyone chattered about their assignments for the day.

When they left in vans for the 30-minute ride to the camps, Elaine approached us with mops and buckets.

"Well, ladies, I thought about your offer of help, and I've come up with a project for you.

"A Vietnamese family that was working with us moved out, and we need to get their house ready for some new volunteers coming next week."

My heart sank when I saw the house. Cobwebs dripped from the ceiling fans, a thick layer of dust covered the furniture, and several months' worth of grease coated the kitchen. We were not looking at a one-day project.

At dinner that night, I noticed that most of the team members stared into space and picked at their food. Elaine came over to us and said, "There was a Level Two alert today. I was planning to go over the evacuation procedures with you tomorrow, but now it can't wait. You have to know what to do in case we're shelled."

"What are you talking about?" I asked. "Are we in some kind of danger?"

"Didn't they brief you in Bangkok? This town is in a war zone."

"What does a Level Two alert mean? Will we have to evacuate?"

"It means that conflict has stepped up in Cambodia. Many of the camps are run by opposing political factions, and are used as training grounds for rebel troops. So they're targets.

"We have to be prepared to evacuate our workers at a moment's notice. That's why we all wear radios."

She looked at our white faces and added, "Try not to worry. You'll get used to it."

Undaunted, I asked Elaine again the next day about our passes.

"It'll be a few more days before I hear anything," she said. "But I'm going to a camp today. I'll drive you around the outside and you can get an idea of how they're set up."

As we approached the camp, Elaine briefed us: "Don't take any pictures of the barbed wire fence, the jail, or any of the feeding sites. It's strictly forbidden."

I was struck by the large number of children who rushed to the fence as we drove by, and motioned for us to take their picture.

"Thirty percent of the camp's population is under the age of five," Elaine said. "They were born here. This is the only life they know."

It was a somber ride back to our house as we thought about the condition of the refugees. I realized that Elaine had already worked here for five years, when most people did well to last one. I was only asking for a few weeks.

We felt the excitement at breakfast a few days later.

"Today is the first time Human Rights Day will be celebrated in the camps," a volunteer told me. "The United Nations is sponsoring it, and all kinds of special activities are planned. It's also the first time we'll be allowed to stay past sunset.

"Even the office staff is coming. And we can bring cameras. Usually it takes more than a month to get a camera pass."

I immediately began looking for Elaine.

"Elaine, do you think we'd be able to get a pass today?" I asked hopefully.

"I already looked into it. They're only issuing passes for official volunteers. Since you're just here for a few weeks, they refused."

"Do you think we'll ever get in?"

"It doesn't look good," she admitted. "Why don't you take the day off and borrow some bikes? The border is only a couple of miles away, and you should see it before you leave. But, be careful...."

We pedaled on red clay paths through quiet, innocent-looking rice fields, their golden hue a sharp contrast to the dark green surrounding trees. The scene should have inspired tranquility, but instead, the closer we came to the border, the more anxious I became.

"How do we know when we reach the border?" I asked.

"I suppose there's some kind of marker. We just can't bicycle into Cambodia without being stopped, can we?"

"Someone was telling me this morning that there's a kind of no-man's-land between the two countries, and it's heavily mined," I said. "This is such a rural area that maybe they don't have any kind of formal border guard. For all we know, we might already be in Cambodia."

Stacy stopped dead in her tracks. A few yards in front of us, a man dressed in black pajamas was holding an automatic weapon. Our hearts pounded as he approached.

When he reached us, he broke into a large grin.

"You American?" he asked.

Stacy blurted impetuously, "You Khmer Rouge?"

He chuckled. "No. Thailand. Come see border camp."

He escorted us to a large clearing at the end of the road. There were several low-lying bamboo huts and a volley-ball net. In a hammock strung between two huts, another pajama-clad soldier was napping. Everyone waved. It was not the reception we had expected.

"Where is no-man's-land?" I asked.

"There." He took us to the edge of the clearing. "Don't go there. Bombs."

He pointed to an area just beyond the clearing. There was nothing to distinguish it from where we'd just been. The red clay path continued on through golden fields as far as we could see.

As we continued to look around, the guards became even friendlier. They allowed us to take all the pictures we wanted, and before we left, we ended up taking turns posing with each of them.

As we rode back, Stacy tried to console me. "You got into a camp in Thailand after all."

10

Counting the Cost (Nanci)

Stacy and I lay on our beds in the Singapore hotel, staring at the ceiling. We could hear people walking by our room and laughing. Somehow, the sound of happy people only made us feel worse.

We had just come through a hotel lobby filled with tourists returning with oversized shopping bags. The contents of any of those bags surely cost more than we lived on for a week, and that thought added to our depression.

"Do you think we'll have any mail tomorrow?" Stacy asked. "I can't believe we haven't even received so much as a Christmas card."

No mail had reached us in Thailand, but when we returned to Singapore, we thought we'd find a big batch waiting. All our family and friends knew that we had to layover here frequently between flights.

"It wouldn't hurt so much if so many people hadn't committed to be actively involved in our mission," I said.

I remembered the enthusiasm of our Bible study group when we first told them about our plans. If it hadn't been for their prayers and backing, we wouldn't be here now.

This was our last stop in "civilization" before we set out for three months in Nepal, India, and Pakistan. We knew we were facing the hardest part of our trip so far.

"Well, while we're here, we've got to put on a few extra pounds. Everyone we've talked to has gotten dysentery in India and lost a lot of weight. You can't afford to do that, so let's start 'beefing up,'" I said.

We were silent for awhile. Then Stacy blurted out, "You know, life would be much simpler if we didn't have this 'call.' It would sure be easier to find a husband, for one thing."

"No kidding. It would've been nice to have some man around today to make our travel arrangements, carry our luggage, and worry about where we'll stay after tonight."

We had only budgeted enough money for one night in a hotel, and our flight didn't leave for five days. I dreaded having to always ask people for favors.

"I'm about ready to pack it in," Stacy confessed.

I was stunned. Stacy, the eternal optimist, never talked like that!

I grabbed a Bible and set it on its spine.

"Come on, Stacy. Let's play Bible roulette."

Grudgingly, she sat up. It was one of her favorites.

I allowed the Bible to fall open. Eyes closed, Stacy pointed to a passage. I read it aloud: "The divisions of the gatekeepers: From the Korahites: Meshelemiah son of Kore, one of the sons of Asaph."

She looked at me with contempt. I tried again. The Bible fell open to Ecclesiastes 10:1-2. This time Stacy read: "As dead flies give perfume a bad smell, so a little folly outweighs wisdom and honor. The heart of the wise inclines to the right, but the heart of the fool to the left."

We put the Bible away.

Our last visit to Singapore had been a scheduled stop to look at the work being done here. We'd made friends at the YWAM base and a local church. The Chinese congregation had made us honorary members.

When we went to church there that night, the pastor, David Stitt, flashed us a smile. His wife Dee, directing the worship band, waved. When others turned around to nod at us, I felt my spirits lift a little. I wondered which one we would have to ask for a place to stay.

David introduced the guest speakers, a missionary couple from Israel. The wife rose to speak. "Before my husband preaches, I feel I must share something that came to me while I was praying about an hour ago. I think it's a message for someone here."

Stacy and I looked at each other. We'd been on our knees about an hour ago, sharing all our loneliness and frustrations with the Lord.

"I think this is for us," Stacy whispered.

"This will be a year for sending people into the harvest," she continued, opening her Bible. "Turn to Psalm 2:8: "Ask of me, and I will make the nations your inheritance...." Then she closed the Bible and looked directly at me. "Those of you who have a call to missions must be obedient to God."

I bolted upright in my seat. God cared enough about Stacy and me to send us a direct message! This was powerful stuff.

After the service, she came up to us. "For some reason," she said, "I feel like I need to talk to you about being single. When I decided to become a missionary, I thought I would never marry because I was always on the move. But God's timing is not the same as ours. When I was in my late 30s and working in South Africa, a wonderful man came for a speaking engagement. That's the man you heard here tonight."

David joined us just then. "What are you doing in Singapore again?" he asked.

"Singapore Airlines only flies to Nepal twice a week. We have to wait here a few days."

"Great," he said. "We have an empty guest house. You can move in tomorrow."

As I climbed into bed that night, I said to Stacy, "What a day! I never thought God would answer our prayers so fast. I can't wait to open our mail tomorrow."

Stacy came out of the YWAM office the next morning, waving two envelopes. We tore into them, dying for news from home. We shook out two Christmas cards. They were each signed with a name and a "smiley face." No personal message. No words of encouragement. No news.

Our spirits lifted a bit when we saw the guest house. It was actually a two-story, three-bedroom home, complete with air conditioning and hot water—items not to take for granted in Asia.

While I unpacked, Stacy cranked up the air conditioner as high as it would go.

"Now that we've got a place to stay, we need to fatten you up," I said to Stacy. No sooner were the words out of my mouth than there was a knock at the door. A young woman we'd met the night before at church was standing in the doorway holding a freshly baked cheesecake.

"It's a welcome gift," she said shyly. "You mentioned that you liked cheesecake."

I rolled my eyes toward the ceiling. I was afraid to ask for anything more.

The next day I started reading up on Nepal. "Hey, Stacy," I called. "Guess what. This says that Kathmandu is 'the hepatitis capital of the world.' And guess what else. We're gonna be there during the height of hepatitis season!"

We were invited to Dee and David's for dinner. As we gathered around the table, David looked at us intently.

"Tell me how you're really doing," he said.

Caught off guard, words tumbled out of my mouth. "Awful. All our friends have forgotten us. They've hardly written. They have no idea how hard this has been."

"I know," David said. "After Dee and I had been here a few months, the mail quit coming. Whenever we go home, everyone's glad to see us. But they have no idea what we really do.

"How about finances?" he asked.

We dodged the issue. I still wasn't comfortable asking for money. The funds in my checking account were rapidly dwindling, but I wasn't panicked yet.

"Hey," he said brightly, "we're having a prayer meeting at 5:00 a.m. tomorrow. Want to come?"

"On Saturday morning?" Stacy asked incredulously. "At 5 a.m.?"

"Sure. A group of us gets together every Saturday morning to pray for the neighborhoods around the church."

I was sure nobody would show up at that time, but we agreed to come to be polite. As we rose to leave, David handed us each an envelope of cash.

"Just to let you know that somebody is still behind you." We hurried out before we broke down in tears.

The next morning, we dressed quickly and arrived at church in pre-dawn blackness. The church was almost full. David divided us into groups, and each group was assigned a section of the neighborhood. We were to pray for our section as we walked up and down the streets.

As we walked, David pointed out some things I hadn't known.

"See that house? That's the home of an Indian couple who go to our church. The red light in the window is supposed to ward off evil spirits. They think I don't know that they still continue some animistic practices. The red light gives them away.

"A friend confessed to me that he knows the spirits he worships are evil, but he prays to the less evil ones to protect him from the more evil ones. I suppose he believes in hedging his bets."

A loud clattering and clanging noise pierced the early morning. As we drew nearer, we could hear that it came from a brightly painted Hindu temple. Along the front of the building were gargoyle-like figures representing members of the Hindu pantheon. An elephant-headed figure with human features eyed us maliciously as we peered inside the temple.

"Why are they making so much noise?" I inquired.

"To wake up their gods. They do it every morning."

I had to laugh. For me, it was the other way around. God often had to wake me up to remind me to spend time with Him.

––––––––––––

We left for Nepal the next morning. The Christmas mail still hadn't arrived, but it didn't seem as important anymore.

"Nanci," Stacy came in as I was zipping my backpack. "I just read a great Scripture. Listen."

She put on her "prophet face" and said, "It's in Matthew: 'And everyone who has left houses or brothers or sisters or father or mother or children or fields for my sake will receive a hundred times as much and will inherit eternal life.'"

We were "beefed up" and ready to go on.

11

A "Drop-in" for "Dropouts" (Stacy)

We were sitting in the Hungry Eye Cafe in Kathmandu, watching candle smoke curl around the room and listening to a recording of "Amazing Grace." I mentioned to Nanci that it looked like most of our companions were desperately in need of grace.

The entrance to the cafe was curtained off with strands of love beads, and the walls were papered with flyers advertising treks, tiger safaris, trips to Tibet, Buddhist meditation courses, fortune tellers, and almost everything else imaginable. I was looking for the invitation to Dilaram House that I knew would be there.

A woman, also heavily decorated with ropes of beads, entered. Finding no empty tables, she took a seat at ours.

"So, how long have you been here?" I asked, making polite conversation.

"About a week. I've found such peace. Such freedom and love," she replied. Nanci and I nodded.

"I'm enrolling in a Buddhist course," she went on. "They teach you how to find the real you within."

A candidate for Dilaram, I thought.

In an attempt to change the subject, I asked where else she'd been. "I spent six weeks in India. They tell you not to drink the water, but no worries," she said. "The secret is to swallow one garlic clove a day, and then you can eat or drink whatever you like. I even drank from the Ganges, where they burn the bodies."

We nodded.

"Let me give you a tip if you go there," she said, lowering her voice and leaning toward us. "If you have any problems waiting in line, start crying and saying loudly, 'I'm pregnant. I'm pregnant.' Indians will move right out of the way for a pregnant woman every time."

"I'll remember that," I said. The music had changed and swelled: "The answer, my friend, is blowing in the wind, the answer is blowing in the wind...."

Nepal opened its borders to the rest of the world in the early 1950s. At first, the amiable Nepalese welcomed the hippies, who quickly became resident "dropouts" in Kathmandu. At that time, Nepal had no drug laws, so hashish and opium could be purchased at produce markets alongside tomatoes and cucumbers. Kathmandu became infamous for Freak Street and its "pie shops," which sold drug-laced baked goods; especially popular were green hashish brownies.

Times changed along with Nepalese tolerance of the drug trade. Drugs are now illegal, although still plentiful. Hippies were replaced by "trekkies." Kathmandu became an Asian mecca for New Age soul-searchers.

Citizens of this tiny country, which is lodged between northern India and Tibet, practice a curious combination of Hinduism and a select form of Buddhism. We came to see how it worked. When we landed, we made our way to the only address we knew: Dilaram House—a refuge for foreigners who'd taken the "wrong turn." From there, we were escorted to a house a mile away to stay with "under-cover" missionaries.

"There's a bathroom through here," the lady who showed us to our bedroom said, pointing to a door with a wooden board leaning against it. "Rap on it a few times before you go in. It'll scare away the rats and the snake that likes to curl up under the sink."

She left us to think about her words. Our response was

to crawl up onto the bed and pull the covers over our heads.

Early the next morning, we headed back down the road to Dilaram to join their morning Bible study. We were greeted by Jenine and Greg, the house directors. Jenine was dressed in a long skirt, and her braided, waist-length hair hung down her back. Greg had bushy, dark brown hair, moustache, and beard. His eyes and mouth crinkled in a perpetual smile.

"We'd like to tell you about Dilaram before the study begins," Jenine said. "Dilaram's a community that cares for travelers in crisis. That's the best way to explain it. A lot of people come to Kathmandu searching for something, but they usually end up disillusioned or strung out on drugs. That's where we step in."

We followed her into a large room with couches, over-stuffed chairs, and beanbags lining the walls. We saw shelves of books on Christianity, philosophy, literature, art, and history. We also saw an assortment of people, all nationalities and ages. But the room was strangely quiet.

Jenine passed out tattered song sheets as Greg tuned his guitar. Then Greg began singing simple Christian songs, much like the ones I had learned as a young girl at church camp. He read a psalm, then led a discussion on communication. Communication was surely needed here.

For lunch, we were served a meal of rice and *dhal bhat* (lentil soup). We were excited to sample the national dish. Little did we know that variations of *dhal bhat* were to be our daily fare for the next three months.

"How do people find out about you?" I asked Jenine.

"Some see the flyers we have around town, inviting them to 'free tea.' The staff also goes to restaurants where likely candidates hang out, and invites them personally to drop in. Some are brought here by their embassies if they are too distraught to return home. Whatever brings them here, they all need a lot of love and time to sort things out.

"All our guests are expected to work, and their names

are placed into the rotation of chores along with the staff,"
Jenine said. "We take care of them until they're able to
return home. We talk to them about God and try to
demonstrate His love, but we don't push them into Christianity. We just provide an environment for them to discover it for themselves."

Jenine gave us a tour of the house. Upstairs was the
"crash room," a bare, padded cubicle for someone in the
midst of a breakdown or drug withdrawal. "Staff members
sit with a person around the clock, if necessary," Jenine
said.

"We encourage people to stay at least a week. Sometimes, though, family members find out they're here and
hire an escort to come get them immediately. It's a big
mistake. Western psychologists have no experience with
patients who've undergone the variety of things these
people have."

She excused herself and went to meet two American
girls who'd just arrived. While she fixed them a pot of tea
and heated leftovers, she carefully questioned them to
determine their situation. When she returned, she told us
they were sick and broke. And scared. I admired her way
of getting information quickly and compassionately.

We continued to go by Dilaram when we weren't busy
with other mission activities. On the way through the
courtyard one day, I stopped to sit beside a woman on a
cement bench in the garden. I'd passed her every day.

We learned that the blind, mute woman's only friends
were the people of Dilaram. Even her family, who lived
down the road, had abandoned her. Each morning, she was
there waiting when the gates opened. One of the staff led
her to the bench. Throughout the day, people came out to
talk to her and feed her. At sunset, they escorted her back
to the gate.

I took the woman's face in my hands, and she smiled

and raised her head toward me. As I gazed into her sight-less eyes, I hoped that she had seen God through the people who cared for her.

I thought about the song we'd heard in the Hungry Eye when we first arrived: "I once was lost, but now I'm found; was blind, but now I see."

———————————

Note: In April, 1989, three months after we left Nepal, the Nepalese government enacted new laws restricting foreign visas for residential status. Despite repeated at-tempts to petition the government for an appeal, Dilaram was forced to close its doors, and its staff was forced to leave the country. We pray God's care over the precious old woman and the thousands of "searchers" passing through Nepal each year who will miss them.

12

Beautiful Feet (Stacy)

The stench of smoldering flesh filled the crisp Himalayan air. Two dirty feet protruded from beneath a mass of burning wood and straw. The body burned for three hours, signaling its departure from this world and its entry into the next.

On a neighboring stone *ghat,* a man brushed ashes into the Bagmati River, the Ganges of Nepal. They were most likely ashes from an affluent Hindu, since the entire body had been consumed by fire. Normally, the poorer classes can't afford enough wood to fully burn a body; what's left is swept into the river to float downstream. It's not uncommon to see assorted arms and legs drifting by as the Bagmati carries reminders of death through town.

I peered 50 yards downriver. Women were doing the family's laundry. Children panned for the gold pieces that are placed in the mouth of a body before cremation. The gold serves both as an offering to the gods and as *baksheesh* to obtain good stature in the next life. I looked again at the ghat; the fire was building, cracking, and sending up bellows of oily smoke.

"Hello, ma'am," a man's voice startled me.

I turned and looked down into the eyes of a bent-over, middle-aged, Nepalese peasant. His face was creased with dirt; his feet were bare. Black whiskers poked out from his chin and cheeks.

"You tourist?" he asked.

"Yes." I paused. "Are you Hindu?"

He didn't respond for a few minutes. We stared, together, at the ceremony below.

"I Christian," he whispered. "Not safe to be Christian here. I go jail six years if people know."

"I'm a Christian, too," I replied boldly.

"Be careful," he said. "Not safe for you, too. Sometimes I go Hindu temple so they think I am Hindu. But afraid to go to church."

I nodded that I understood. He bowed and left.

Across the river, Pashupatinath, Nepal's holiest Hindu temple, rose above the low bank. It is dedicated to Shiva, the guardian spirit of Nepal. Non-Hindus are forbidden entrance to the temple compound.

Shiva is a patron god known as both Destroyer and Creator. He's often depicted as a light-skinned man with a blue throat, five faces, four arms, and three eyes. In his arms he holds a trident, a sword, a bow, and a skull. At times, he soars through the air on a bull, accompanied by his elephant-headed son Ganesh.

Nanci and I continued to observe the ceremonial burning, caught between our curiosity and our desire to escape the foul odor. I squirmed as bystanders worked themselves into a frenzy in front of the burning bodies, flailing their arms and legs, chanting.

Each morning, Nanci and I watched the Nepalese make their way to temples for their daily *puja,* or offering. They carried small, metal plates stacked with grains of rice, red powder, and tiny yellow flower petals. The contents were scattered on idols, while drums pounded to ensure that the gods paid attention. Afterward, the offerings were mixed with bits of clay to form a sticky substance, and a small dot of the mixture was placed on the worshiper's forehead between the eyes. This is called *tika,* a symbol of the presence of the divine.

Some people spent their entire morning going from

temple to temple, performing *pujas*. Others stopped randomly throughout the day to pick up a dab of the red powder mixture and brush it across their forehead, leaving grains of rice sticking out in strange patterns. They did this to ensure continual protection. What wasn't picked up by people was often picked at by stray dogs and sacred cows roaming the streets.

We'd come to Nepal to meet with local Christians and foreign missionaries involved in covert work, whose stories we had heard in the United States.

The residence where we were staying was known to the police, who would periodically "drop in" for tea. Had they wanted to arrest everyone there, they could have.

"Hide your interview notes, tapes, and journals," the house director warned us. "There's a joke among the missionaries that if you don't get arrested for 'working' in Nepal, you weren't 'working' very hard.

"Our former director has been deported so many times that his picture is displayed at the airport. He's forbidden reentry. He still sneaks in periodically, though. We're praying he'll make it for the pastor's conference."

He stopped suddenly.

"Pretend you didn't hear that," he said. "It's best that you know nothing about it.

"Let me show you something," he said, and began digging through stacks of paper. "About six weeks ago, two Americans were arrested and sentenced to three years in jail. It was Jeff's third arrest in as many visits to Nepal. He and Scott were picked up for distributing Christian literature and Bibles in a remote area of the Himalayas. Jeff's journal was seized by the police to use as evidence against him, but we were able to get an excerpt from it."

He handed us a mimeographed page:

Of all the treks I've done, this was the best one.
We distributed over 1,500 books. There are few known

believers among the Sherpas, but I think we found a few more who were previously unknown.

"Just yesterday, we received a letter Jeff was able to sneak out. Here's an excerpt from it."

Having heard about the torture prisoners receive at the hands of the police, it was still heartrending to see it firsthand. A fellow inmate suffered permanent brain damage as the result of a beating. Police club the soles of the feet to a pulp, smash heads against the wall, shove pins underneath fingernails and toenails, administer electric shocks, and more.

"Why?" was all I could ask.

"Nepalese law states: 'No person shall propagate Christianity, Islam, or any other faith so as to disrupt the traditional religion of the Hindu community of Nepal.' Conversion from Hinduism carries a one-year jail sentence. Evangelism resulting in a conversion draws three years, and baptizing a new believer means six years in jail.

"The problem for the government is that Christianity is growing at a phenomenal rate. From 1981 to 1984, the government admitted an increase from 4,000 to over 30,000 Christians. Non-governmental figures estimate it even higher. The queen was so upset that she asked the king for only one thing for her birthday in 1988: that 'Nepal remain a Hindu kingdom.'"

We looked forward to interviewing our official contact, a young Nepalese evangelist named Mirendah. Tales of his courage were legendary. He and his co-worker Bhimsen invited us to tea soon after our arrival.

The house where Mirendah, Bhimsen, and Bhimsen's wife Sita lived had few amenities. There was no electricity. The second story wasn't even roofed yet. Mirendah showed us to one of their three nearly bare rooms. We placed our cassette recorder on the table and began interviewing them. Mirendah's English was better than

Bhimsen's, so most of our conversation was with him.

We talked about their work in villages outside Kathmandu. We asked to visit a church they had started, but were told it could endanger the Christians living there.

"How did you start church planting?" Nanci asked.

"I had been fasting and praying for days. Then God put on my heart the verse from Isaiah 52:7: 'How beautiful on the mountains are the feet of those who bring good news...who proclaim salvation....'

"At the same time, I received a vision of the foothills of the Himalayas. I knew that my ministry was to be in the mountains of Nepal."

I whispered to Nanci that this was the same verse that had inspired Jacqui in the Philippines.

For over an hour, we listened to Mirendah describe the difficulties involved in his first attempt to establish a church. "In September of 1986, I hiked into Bunghit and began talking with a group of young men. I briefly told them about Jesus, but had to hurry away before the police showed up. I promised to return.

"I went back about once a week. Each time, they asked more questions. Then finally, after months of work, five men met me outside the village on my way in. They said that they wanted to accept Jesus. That was the beginning of the church in Bunghit.

"Then one day, a group of older men broke into our meeting. They chased me from the village and warned, 'Never come back here, or we will kill you.' So I discipled the new Christians by mail until I thought it safe to return.

"As I approached the village, some of the Christians came running toward me, shouting. I thought they were telling me to stay away. But they were so excited that they were babbling all at once. They said that two nights earlier, the band of men who had threatened me had mysteriously left. They never returned."

Bhimsen jumped in, "Eleven years ago, two foreign

women came to my village. They told us of Jesus, and my entire family became Christians. But we had to leave our village. It wasn't safe to live there anymore."

Mirendah's last story had no ending. Two Nepalese men began a small fellowship in a mountain community. Then one day they were threatened with death if they ever returned. Just two weeks before our visit, they showed up in Kathmandu and prayed with Mirendah and other Christians for guidance. They asked if they should offer themselves as martyrs. Believing they were to return, they did.

"They've not been heard from since," Mirendah said.

"Are you afraid of the police?" I asked.

"No. They try to scare us. They come to our churches and beat us to remind us who's in charge. But we know that Jesus will take care of us."

"One last question," I asked before we left. "What's the greatest need in Nepal?"

"Trained church leaders," they both agreed.

Back at the mission house, the other Americans staying there had made a big decision: they needed a break from the endless diet of rice and lentils.

"We'll take care of it," the men said.

"Indian takeout," whispered one of their wives.

Indian "food to go" was very popular, although done with a different twist. The men rode off on mountain bikes with bags of plastic containers (Styrofoam had yet to reach Nepal). They rode past streetside vendors, buying chicken *tikka* from one, *rotis* from another, and curried vegetables from still another, until a full meal was acquired.

We sat on the floor, scooping everything up using *rotis* (flat round Indian bread) as our silverware, making sure to eat only with our right hand. (The left is used for other things in a country where toilet paper is a rarity and a cultural curiosity.) Each person discussed his day's activities: contacts made, prayer meetings held, and preparations for the conference.

I was humbled as I looked around the room at our housemates, people who risked everything to live here and work for the Lord.

We set aside one day to explore Kathmandu. As our guidebook said, "The valley consists of as many temples as there are houses, and as many idols as there are men." The temples are made of wood well into the decay process, and are overgrown with moss and weeds. Monkeys scavenge in and around the grounds of the larger temples, and even attempt to raid visitors' belongings.

For hours, we wound through a maze of dark streets and hidden alleys, where tightly clustered buildings permitted only tiny slits of light to seep through. Each street had its own assortment of sunken fountains, temples, idols, and secret passageways.

The Nepalese went about their daily chores with no sense of urgency. Children played in the dirt and fountains with anything they could use as a toy. I saw one toddler playing with the bloody head of a slaughtered buffalo.

Occasionally, we passed a butcher who whispered, "Have beef. Want beef?" It was illegal to kill cows, but some Nepalese took the risk for the great profits it brought.

At one point, we climbed the crowded steps of a temple and sat to rest in the high mountain sunshine. A man instantly appeared and handed me a piece of paper. It read: "I would like to clean your ears. Good price."

I showed the note to Nanci, who looked horrified, and we both shook our heads. He pulled out a little note pad and offered it to me. It contained pages of recommendations by satisfied customers.

On our last night in Nepal, we were picked up by a taxi and driven to an unknown destination. Waiting in the taxi was an American woman. She steadied large pots of *chai* (tea boiled with milk and sugar) on the floor and in her lap. We rode along in silence.

At the end of a dirt road, the taxi stopped. We got out and followed the woman into the courtyard of a small L-shaped building. (Churches are often L-shaped in Nepal so anyone looking in can only see half the congregation.)

It was the first night of the four-day pastor's conference we'd heard so much about. This was a historic event—the first of its type to take place in Nepal. All arrangements had been handled with the utmost secrecy. Each evening, the meetings moved to a different location, announced only that day to a select few.

"Did he make it?" Mirendah asked the woman with us.

"We don't know yet. He knows where we'll be."

I decided they were talking about the former director of the house where we'd been staying.

We'd arrived early to set up tea and cookies. Soon pastors began to assemble. As I served them cups of *chai*, I remembered the last words of our interview with Mirendah and Bhimsen, "We need more trained leaders." This was the answer to their prayers.

"I'm Pastor Dureddy," an older man said, smiling at me as I ladled him a cup of *chai*. "I've been arrested 17 times, but no more." He proudly pulled from his Bible a crumpled piece of paper with an official seal.

"This is an order from the king of Nepal that says I can never be arrested again."

There was an outburst in a corner of the courtyard. Two men had just arrived. I rushed to see what was happening.

"These are the men I told you about," Mirendah exclaimed, rushing past us and extending his arms. It turned out that these were the two men who had been threatened with death if they ever returned to their village. They were not only accepted in the village, but the people were so impressed by their courage that they wanted to learn more about their faith. They had been too busy preaching the Gospel to report back to Kathmandu!

A few minutes later, a thin, scruffy man with dark brown hair and a full beard entered the compound. He looked to me like a candidate for Dilaram. But when Mirendah spied him, he was overcome with joy.

Nanci and I both smiled. The ex-director had made it. He'd disguised himself and gotten through immigration.

The meeting lasted for hours. Then we served a traditional Nepalese feast, catered by students from an undercover Christian training school. With no cooking facilities at the church, they had brought the complete meal in bits and pieces by foot, bikes, motorcycles, and taxis.

The police could have stormed in at any minute and arrested us all, except the old pastor, of course. But I felt strangely protected, like God was looking at us, smiling.

Note: After 125 days, Jeff and Scott were put on trial and charged with preaching Christianity. The courtroom served as a forum for spreading the Gospel, since it was entered as evidence. Although the judge wanted to sentence them to a full three-year term, he was under pressure from the United States to release them. The U.S. government was forced into action when it received hundreds of letters from American Christians lobbying for their freedom. They were acquitted and immediately deported.

Note: In spite of major breakthroughs in establishing both political and religious freedom in Nepal since the uprisings of April, 1990, the situation there is still volatile enough that we changed the names of persons and locations in this chapter.

13

Cups of Cool Water (Nanci)

When we entered Calcutta, I remembered that Rudyard Kipling had described it as the "city of dreadful night." I had to agree with him.

The headlights of our taxi seemed to fight their way through the smoky twilight as we merged into a steady stream of traffic. Even with the windows tightly closed, dirt seeped in and plastered itself to our skin and clothes. Cooking fires along the street lit up the night. My eyes burned, and I choked slightly with each breath. The air seemed permeated with human want and suffering.

This was our introduction to India.

We were met at Dum Dum Airport by a Filipino YWAM worker named Manny. We barely had time for proper greetings before he hustled us off to a taxi.

"You'll be heading straight to Uluberia, a half-hour train ride from here," he said.

We were going to Howrah, the largest train station in the world. I had known we'd have to face the infamous place at some point, but hoped it wouldn't be so soon. Even travelers in China had warned us about it. Howrah's huge permanent population includes families who eat, sleep, and live on its platforms. Crime and disease run rampant.

Manny noticed our anxious glances. "Don't worry," he said. "I plan to stay with you all the way."

The driver turned and said something which Manny interpreted. "Keep your eyes on the car trunk. When traffic stops, thieves pry them open and steal what's inside."

Stacy and I turned so we could glare menacingly at anyone who came near, not an easy task given the crowds pressed against the sides of the taxi. We sat that way for the rest of the ride.

Howrah lived up to its reputation. The air reeked of stale urine and of unwashed bodies lying on the pavement as haphazardly as scattered leaves. Vacant-eyed children, too tired to stand, held out their palms for rupees. Water vendors and food peddlers wandered through the crowd, hawking their wares. All the while, the public address system bellowed announcements to a seemingly uninterested audience.

I stuck close to Manny, and clutched my luggage to my body as he navigated us to our train. The air was so hot that we fought to catch our breath.

"This is a ladies' compartment," he explained. "You'll be safer here. I have to ride in the men's compartment, but I'll come get you when it's time to get off."

Women in brightly colored saris were engrossed in sewing and conversation. Vendors wound their way up and down the narrow aisles selling hair ribbons, *tilaks* (colored dots Indian women wear on their foreheads), fruits, and nuts. The compartment doors were propped open to permit fresh air and new arrivals to enter.

I was glad when Manny came to retrieve us.

He led us to a bicycle ricksha, and gave instructions to the driver in Bengali. "I'll follow with your luggage," he said, and we set off into a now pitch-black night along a dirt road, without the slightest idea where we were going.

"Do you think we're safe?" Stacy whispered. Stacy always had a sense of drama. I was determined not to let her fears affect me.

Finally, the ricksha stopped in front of a two-story house, and we waited outside until Manny pulled up in another ricksha. He led us into the house, and introduced us to the team living there.

The next morning, Maddy, the Chinese lady from California who was the team leader, explained the nature of the team's ministry. They provided primary health care for a Bangladeshi refugee camp, a tiny village near the YWAM house. The refugees were Moslems who fled their country after the war of independence in 1971, when East Pakistan broke away from Pakistan and was renamed Bangladesh.

"However, since you don't have any medical training," Maddy said, "you'll be working with an Indian couple named Dolly and Lablu Baroi in the children's ministry. But if you want to, you can join our health classes twice a week and then go out with us to see what it's like."

Stacy's eyes lit up. She had started college as a premed student. Anything having to do with the health field intrigued her.

"We're studying how to diagnose and treat dysentery," Maddy said. "Next week, I'll teach everyone how to do a basic exam." Since Stacy was wildly imaginative and a bit of a hypochondriac, I just knew she would think she had some terrible tropical disease after each class.

It was hard to believe that 15 team members lived in the three-bedroom, one-bath house. One of the bedrooms had even been vacated for us to use.

"We do have running water, but it only comes on three times a day," Maddy said. "Be sure and add water to the plastic garbage cans in the kitchen whenever they're low. It's our emergency supply for flushing toilets and washing dishes when the water is off.

"We don't have any hot water, but you can put an electric coil in a bucket and heat some for a bucket shower. It takes about half an hour. Just be sure to unplug it before you stick your hand in to check the temperature. We've lost a few people who forgot."

I smiled. I was delighted at the prospect of my first hot "shower" in months, regardless of the hazards.

That afternoon, we met Dolly and Lablu. "We have a Bible club every afternoon for the refugee children," Dolly told us. "They're so poor that they can't afford to go to school, and there's nothing for them to do around here. We teach them Bible stories and Christian songs. Even though they're Hindu or Muslim, their parents let them come. We give them a short English lesson, and we play games."

"Can you start tomorrow?" she asked hopefully.

Dolly helped us find appropriate clothing to wear, since the villagers spurned Western attire. We weren't up to tackling saris yet, because draping them required a certain degree of finesse. Nothing seemed worse than tripping over one's sari and having it unravel. So Dolly found us some *punjabis,* knee-length tunics over baggy pants, which discreetly covered our ankles.

Several children grabbed our hands as we walked over to the shaded churchyard where the meetings were held. Dolly started the meeting with a prayer and an unexpected introduction.

"This is Stacy and Nanci," she announced. "They're going to sing a song for you." Stacy looked at me, terrified. She hated to sing in public.

"I'll carry you," I whispered. "Just stand beside me." I sang as loudly as I could to drown out Stacy's shaky voice, and we managed to get through it. It was a big hit with the kids.

Almost all the children, even many of the boys, wore thick black eyeliner around their coal-black eyes. The children were obviously unwashed, and several of the younger ones were naked from the waist down. When it was game time, the children crowded around us and begged for piggyback rides. Our backs almost gave out, but before the afternoon was over, we were a success.

"It's time for our clinic," Dolly announced, and the children eagerly gathered around her. Most of them received no medical attention at home for cuts and scrapes.

Even though their wounds usually weren't serious, they could become dangerously infected.

Dolly taught us the routine. As each child came forward, either Stacy or I prayed for healing, then applied antiseptic and a bandage. The treatment was finished with a hug. Although they didn't know it, I added a few extra prayers for each one.

One boy came to me, pointing to a knee injury which had been healed for weeks. I prayed for him anyway, put on a bandage, and gave him the biggest hug of the day. He was still smiling when he skipped away.

The day came when we were invited to join the medical team on their rounds in the refugee village. First-aid kits in hand, we tagged along behind Maddy and the other nurses. The villagers lived in dried mud houses with ceilings so low that, even the short natives couldn't stand fully upright. Cows, sheep, and goats ambled along the dirt paths between houses. As we passed by, people called for us to treat someone in their household. Some stopped Maddy just to exchange small talk or to ask her advice about family problems.

Stacy and I filled out medical records and passed out bandages. We prayed with the team for each person before treatment was administered. Sometimes Philip, the team evangelist, left a tract in Bengali.

Maddy diagnosed one boy as suffering from a vitamin A deficiency, and quickly gave him a megadose. "If we'd waited even one more day, he probably would have been permanently blind," she sighed. "Vitamin A deficiency is one of the most common health problems in developing nations. It's easily treatable if it's caught in time."

We made rounds until it was too dark to work any longer, and when we returned, the staff was all abuzz.

"We've been invited to a wedding this Friday. We've been working here a year, and this is the first time we've been invited to anything. It's a real breakthrough," Maddy said.

Stacy and I had no idea what an unusual role we were going to play in that wedding.

The day of the wedding coincided with our last day with the team, so Dolly had a special surprise for us.

"See these saris?" she said. "Pick one out, and you can wear it to the Bible club. I'll show you how they work."

I found a black one that looked long enough to fit me. Stacy chose a white floral. Then Dolly handed us each a white midriff blouse to wear under our saris.

"Make sure my stomach is covered," I reminded her. "In the United States, it's not as acceptable to show one's midriff."

We all laughed. In India, ladies had no qualms about displaying their abdomens, but they thought it offensive to wear sleeveless blouses or pants that were remotely tight.

"Don't worry," Dolly quipped. "I'll make sure we wouldn't upset your mommy." (Indians referred to their mothers as mommies.)

We practiced hobbling around in our saris before we dared venture out in public. As we carefully made our way to the Bible club, the villagers lined up to watch us, and each nodded his head in approval. It was inconceivable to them that any woman wouldn't prefer wearing a sari.

We didn't expect many children that day, because most of them were either involved in the wedding preparations or were participating in a Hindu *puja* (religious celebration) for the goddess of education. So we planned a special activity; we decided to give them a lesson in applying makeup. It was a huge success. Even the boys loved watching it. They teased the girls mercilessly, and their laughter could be heard throughout the village.

Word spread quickly about what we were doing. Within minutes, one of the local women came and asked Dolly if we would be willing to make up the bride. Before we knew it, we were being ushered to the bride's home.

We were led to a sad-faced young woman sitting on a banana leaf mat outside a small mud hut.

"The bride is supposed to pretend she is mourning because she has to leave her parents' home for her husband's," Dolly whispered in my ear. "Even though the groom only lives next door, it wouldn't be proper for her to show any joy."

Stacy assisted as I nervously spread on blush, eye shadow, and mascara, hoping my ineptitude wouldn't cause the young woman further grief.

"When's the wedding?" Stacy asked casually.

"Whenever you finish," was the answer.

At that, even though no one else seemed in a hurry, I sped up the process. This was one aspect of mission work I hadn't trained for.

When I had done my best, Dolly added artful designs to the bride's forehead with yellow paint.

Then we were pressed for further service. The bride's family had noticed us taking pictures on several occasions. They asked if we would be the official wedding photographers. Fortunately, we were already dressed in saris, so we needed only to retrieve our cameras.

We were escorted to seats of honor in a large clearing under a banana leaf canopy. The wedding party and village elders sat on a carpet of banana leaves. The bride wore a traditional red wedding sari with intricate designs worked in gold thread. The groom wore a white T-shirt and what looked like white pajama bottoms. Everyone had very solemn expressions.

The officiating priest lightly bound the bride and groom's wrists together with a white cloth. Then they walked slowly arm-in-arm around a small fire. The bride was handed a coconut to drop into the fire. Periodically, a relative tapped one of us on the shoulder when it was time to snap a picture.

When the ceremony was over, we were invited to a house where the bride and groom were receiving guests. I was quietly sipping tea when I noticed that several people were pointing at me and making animated gestures. An old woman came over and wound the end of my sari over my head. Then two other people grasped my elbows and led me to where the bride was visiting with friends. Everyone began smiling and chattering excitedly. Finally, one of the guests explained to me: "We all think you look exactly like Indira Gandhi!"

I tried to look pleased. I was sure they meant it as a compliment. Besides, it was the first emotion I had seen since the beginning of the wedding.

The next morning, we returned to Calcutta.

Howrah Station was less intimidating this time, and we confidently made our way outside and hailed a taxi to take us to the Baptist guest house where we were scheduled to spend a few days.

As we drove there, I thought about Calcutta's former glory. Founded three hundred years earlier by the British on the banks of the Hooghly River, Calcutta was once the most cosmopolitan city in India. Until 1911, it served as India's capital, and under colonial rule, was considered one of the "crown jewels" of the British Empire. Few remnants remained of her former splendor.

Since India gained its independence in 1947, the city has undergone steady decline. With every political upheaval or natural disaster (during monsoon season India falls prey to murderous typhoons), the population of the city swells with refugees from the countryside. Although Calcutta was originally built to accommodate 200,000 to 300,000 people, over 9 million currently live there, many of them homeless.

For years, experts from around the world have predicted the final collapse of this city. But Calcutta defies them all and tenaciously clings to life.

The neighborhood around our guest house waited to be explored. Sacred cows, scrawny piebald dogs, goats, pigs, and sheep wandered at will. As we turned one corner, we bumped into a group of men bathing themselves while doing their laundry in a broken water main. Rows of dingy gray clothes were spread over cement walls to dry. A barber wielded his rusty tools inside a dusty alley. Shoe salesmen, bicycle repairmen, snake charmers, beggars, and food vendors lined the road.

As we passed a snake vendor, he lifted the top of his basket and the head of a cobra popped out. I grabbed my camera and he said, "One rupee?" When I shook my head, the lid slammed back down.

We came upon a line of ricksha *wallahs* (drivers) patiently waiting for customers. These *wallahs* trot through heavy traffic pulling passengers in clumsy wooden carts.

"I read that most of these men die from sheer exhaustion before they're 40," I told Stacy. "Their bodies are so worn down that they contract tuberculosis or some other disease.

"And they think they're the lucky ones; they have jobs. They actually fight for the privilege of pulling a ricksha."

The next morning, we ran into an American mission team that was volunteering at Mother Teresa's House for the Destitute and Dying. Hundreds come to work there each year. Some are Christians; some just humanitarians.

The home is located in one of the city's worst slums, next door to a temple dedicated to Kali, the goddess of death and destruction and Calcutta's patron "saint." Legend has it that when the goddess was dismembered, her toe fell where Calcutta is today. All that existed before the British came was a shrine to commemorate the event.

As we approached Mother Teresa's, we heard wails and screams coming from the temple. Mother Teresa's workers had told us that their worship often consisted of terrible acts of appeasement—animals and an occasional infant being sacrificed to stave off Kali's wrath.

"I'm not sure if I can go on," I said. "I think I've seen about enough suffering for one day."

Just then, a girl from the American team came by and offered to take us into Mother Teresa's house and show us the routine.

There was one room for women and one for men. Each room had two tiers, with 50 beds on each tier.

"The bottom tier," the girl explained, "is for those closest to death."

Quotations from Jesus and various saints were stenciled on the walls. Parakeets roosted in some of the alcoves above the dark green cots, their songs providing a marked contrast to the somberness of the surroundings. The rooms were plain, but clean, and devoid of any of the paraphernalia associated with modern hospitals.

A nun greeted us by handing each of us an apron.

"Let me tell you about the home before you start to work," she said. "We take care of about 200 patients on the verge of dying. Each morning, some of the sisters drive through the streets and bring back people who can't take care of themselves anymore. It doesn't matter what religion they are; they are all God's children. We try to give them a little comfort and love before they die. Our goal is to help them die with dignity."

"Do any recover?" Stacy asked.

"Rarely."

With that, she escorted us to the kitchen, where a number of volunteers were busy doing the breakfast dishes. She handed us a gray rag and pointed to a container full of ashes.

"We don't have soap, so we scrub the dishes with those. Make sure you rinse them well."

Stacy and I squatted on the cold cement floor along with the other workers. I pressed my damp rag into the ashes and scoured the metal plates. It sounded like sandpaper scraping against wood. We rinsed them under a faucet that was only two feet above the ground, and stacked them on the floor to dry.

After we'd been doing this for some time, Stacy tugged on my shirt and silently pointed. Following her gaze, I saw an empty stretcher being carried into the women's section. A few minutes later, the stretcher came back through. It had a body on it.

When we finished our work, we went to find the nun.

"What can we do next?" I asked.

"Well, you can either help bathe the women or wash down their beds and change the sheets."

"We'll do the beds," I said quickly. It was an easy decision. I'd never bathed a sick person before. I was terrified of dropping one and having to watch her being carried away on a stretcher.

While Stacy and I remade the bed, its occupant watched us through glassy eyes from a small chair nearby. When she moved closer to inspect our work, I noticed the skin hanging loosely from her frail yellowed arms. When she opened her mouth, I could see a number of gaps where teeth had once been. Her hair was very thin and pulled back starkly to reveal a face that already had begun to look skeletonized.

Nonetheless, she made sure that we smoothed out every rough spot in her bed before she agreed to return to it. We realized that this was one small aspect of her life over which she still felt she had control.

As we walked to the next bed, I had a chance to examine the room. Volunteers moved around offering physical assistance, prayers, and gentle words. A continual battle was waged to keep the smell of the room from overpowering everyone, but it was ultimately a losing battle due to the odor of rotting flesh and incontinent dying patients. The volunteers appeared to have no worries concerning their own health and the contagious diseases they were coming in contact with.

Loud tuberculin coughs resounded in the room and an almost inaudible sigh or moan seem to hang in the air.

I could barely stand to look at the women in the beds. It was impossible to guess their ages, but they all looked very old and emaciated from bouts of dysentery or years of living on the streets. Everywhere there was a quiet sense of acceptance. They knew there was only one way for them to leave that place.

When Stacy and I finished our work, I wandered around and talked with some of the patients. I sat for a long time just holding the hand of a lady near death. She was too weak to speak. As I rose to leave, I looked at the verse that was inscribed over her bed: "Whatever you did for one of the least of these brothers of mine, you did for me."

14

Kaleidoscope (Nanci)

My first impression of India was that it was like a giant kaleidoscope. Just when I thought I had all its facets neatly pegged, something shifted, and I had to readjust my focus.

We decided to travel by train to get a better picture of the country. I watched with amazement as the frail porter knelt down and hoisted all our bags onto his head. He placed one on top of another on his dirty turban. Inching up, he steadied the bags with one hand and disappeared into the dense crowd.

"Where'd he go?" Stacy kept asking, bobbing up and down. She was so short that she always depended on me to look out for everything.

I caught a glimpse of a blue backpack, and followed it all the way to our car on the Coramandel Express, the fastest train from Calcutta to Madras (27 hours). It had "Second Class Aircon" written on its side. The porter pointed to a list of names pasted on it.

"There we are," I said proudly, "between Mr. Gupta and the Singh family: 28A and B."

Few Indians traveled in sleeper cars because of the cost. Most chose second or third class with hard seats. Weighed down with possessions, they often swayed in the aisles of the crowed cars for hours, waiting for a seat to open up. Theft was rampant. We'd been warned that if we traveled by train, we should chain our bags to our wrists and then to the seat.

Unlike the other cars we'd passed, ours was reasonably

clean and uncrowded. Each compartment held six people, who sat on two long seats facing each other during the day. Each seat had a berth above it. In the corridor outside each compartment, there was a bench seat with a berth over it. These were folded down only at night, when people did not need to walk through the train corridor. Two people from each compartment were assigned to sleep in the hall corridor at night. Stacy and I were grateful that we didn't get that assignment. I reached up to feel the air vents. Thankfully, cool air was coming out.

"You don't need to worry about anything," the porter assured us. "The conductors lock this car at night." Once we were underway, I had a chance to look around the compartment. Our companions were a young Indian couple with two children, two elderly men, and another man who seemed to be traveling alone.

I pulled my Bible from underneath the seat and began reading. I felt someone staring at me. It was the lone traveler, eyeing my Bible. I continued to read, but after a few minutes, he was unable to contain himself any longer. He snatched my Bible from my knees and began leafing through it. Startled, I braced myself for his next move.

"Are you a Christian?" he asked.

"Yes."

"I'm a Hindu. What are you doing in India?"

Unsure of how much I should say, I softly replied, "I'm a missionary."

"That's interesting. Why do you want to change people's religion?" He wasn't argumentative, just curious.

"I want people to know the truth about God," I explained. I didn't know exactly what to say to a Hindu.

"Well, in my religion there are over three million gods. We believe your Jesus was a god, too. But you're just a Christian because you were born in America. I'm a Hindu because I was born in India. It's *karma*.

"We believe that a person is reborn many times before

attaining spiritual perfection. Each time a man is born, he has to pay for the evil he did in his previous life. It is hoped that, if he is growing spiritually, each time he comes back he's reborn into a better set of circumstances."

"Let me see if I understand," I said. "You believe that a poor person deserves to be poor because of sins he committed in his previous life?"

"That's right. A person's circumstances are an indication of his spirituality. A Brahman [a member of the highest caste] has made more progress than an untouchable.

"The goal of each rebirth is to strip away another layer of illusion that man is separate from god. A person eventually reaches the highest state possible—he merges with the god-force that is in everyone and everything."

"I know some Hindus who have become Christians," I told him.

"Impossible. Hindus are born Hindus and they die Hindus."

I decided to give up on this one.

———————

As we stood in the Madras train station, another commuter rushed by and took my last tract. I searched the crowd for Raga, the young Indian missionary who'd invited Stacy and me to help him pass out tracts. I waved that I needed more, but he said there were none left.

"Raga, the tracts went so quickly! People even stuck their hands out the window and grabbed tracts as the train pulled away. Most Americans refuse to take tracts. They won't even accept coupons for free merchandise," I said.

People pushed and shoved to get tracts from us.

Our host told us there's more openness to Christianity in Madras than anywhere else in India. Perhaps because the apostle Thomas was martyred here."

"Raga, were you raised in a Christian family?"

He laughed. "Oh no, I was a devout Hindu. In fact, I was the first person in my community to become a Christian. When my parents heard, they took me to a swami.

"Swamis are considered gods, and people go to them for spiritual advice. A person can become one simply by declaring that he is. Anyway, my parents hoped he would talk some sense into me. Once he found out that my faith was genuine, he confided to me that he also believed in the Bible. However, he made so much money as a swami that he couldn't afford to announce his Christianity."

Our two weeks in Madras passed quickly, and before we knew it, we were on a train for Bombay. It was my turn to take the upper berth. Down below, Stacy was engrossed in a conversation with a young Muslim family.

"Well, we're Muslims because we were born Muslims," the wife said.

I had heard this somewhere before. I decided to let Stacy go it alone.

"The most important thing is to follow the religion you are born into the best way you can," the woman continued.

Stacy hesitated and then tactfully countered, "I think if a person is really sincere in finding God and searches for Him with his whole heart, God is faithful to show him the true way...."

As I drifted off to sleep, I could still hear them arguing.

Our first assignment in Bombay was to help out in the mission base office. Stacy produced a long-overdue newsletter while I wrote a building proposal to a businessman interested in making a sizable donation to the local mission.

Bombay was a microcosm of India, a major economic center second only to Hollywood in the production of movies. People flocked here to seek their fortune; most had their dreams shattered. Surprisingly, the homeless situation seemed as bad as in Calcutta.

On our way to a church meeting, we were stopped by a gang of boys, faces painted in demonic patterns, screeching hideously and whipping themselves with braided ropes that resembled snakes. They rushed up to a pedestrian standing near us, whipping themselves repeatedly until the intimidated onlooker gave them money.

At the next corner, we noticed a disturbance at a line of auto-rickshas. Tall, sari-clad beggars were making their way from ricksha to ricksha, collecting large sums of money. These were the most accomplished beggars I'd ever seen. We knew they were eunuchs, because we had heard of these men who wore women's saris, long wigs, and bright red lipstick.

The locals had told us about the function eunuchs perform in the Hindu religion. They serve as scapegoats, in the Old Testament sense of the word. When babies are born, a eunuch is called to pray for the child. As the eunuch places his hands on the baby, all the sins from the child's previous life are transferred to the eunuch. People always responded to their begging, because to deny eunuchs their only source of income was to court disaster. The curse of a eunuch is considered particularly dire.

We'd been in Delhi almost a week, and most of our time had been spent traipsing back and forth to the Pakistani embassy. Stacy, whose passport had an Israeli stamp in it from a previous trip to Israel, was having difficulty obtaining a visa for Pakistan.

New Delhi reminded me of Washington, D.C., and made me homesick. There were wide, tree-lined boulevards, modern buildings with lawns and gardens, and sparkling clean monuments.

We hired an auto-ricksha to visit Old Delhi and the Red Fort. Booking a ricksha for an entire afternoon was no problem; our driver was happy to have guaranteed work. Because of the abundance of rickshas, most drivers spent more time waiting than driving.

Once in the old city, the streets were so clogged that we were forced to abandon our transportation and proceed on foot anyway, twisting our way around astrologers' booths on the sidewalk, cows sprawled in the middle of the road, and bands of musicians vying to see who could play the loudest, if not the best.

After a long walk, we found the mosque we had come so far to see. There was a huge sign on its iron gate, lauding the martyrdom of Muslims killed in an earlier skirmish with neighboring Hindus.

A guard barred our entrance.

"No women," he barked. We had to settle for a peek through the fence.

We let our driver take us to the other religious shrines. At the Jain temple, men with veils over their mouths stood in groups.

"They believe it's wrong to kill any living thing," our driver explained. "They wear veils so they don't accidentally inhale a gnat or anything."

At the Sikh temple, men with multi-colored turbans were selling flowers to be presented as offerings to the deities inside.

"Why do they all wear turbans?" I asked our driver.

"It's against their religion for men to cut their hair, so they wind it around the top of their head and cover it with a turban."

I sighed. So many traditions, religions, and rules. I'd seen all the parts of India, and still couldn't fit them together.

15

Easter Dupes (Nanci)

"How do I look?" I asked Stacy as we prepared for our flight to Pakistan.

"Terrible! No man would dream of touching you," Stacy assured me.

Stacy and I had taken great pains with our attire, and were pleased with the result. Dressed in long shirts and baggy pants, we looked more like tents than women. We discussed covering our hair, but decided against it.

The clothes we'd chosen were modest by Indian standards, but we knew that Pakistan's dress code would be even more strict, since it was a Muslim country.

Our ability to adapt had grown enormously. We now pulled cultures on and off as quickly as we changed clothes.

After a short flight to Lahore, we boarded a Japanese minivan bound for Gujranwala, an hour away. These vans were popular modes of transportation, and were operated like buses. Our van belonged to the Flying Coach company, aptly named if our driver was typical.

We were on our way to visit Pat Stock, a former housemate who'd recently married an American missionary to Pakistan. Her husband Paul was the boarding master at a Christian vocational school for more than 300 boys under the age of 18.

From what Pat had written us, women were second-class citizens in Pakistan. In one letter, she mentioned that a woman couldn't sit by a man on a bus or van, unless the man was her husband or a close relative. She said that one time when she was traveling alone, she wasn't allowed on a minivan because all the empty seats were next to men. She had to wait for the next van.

We selected our seats carefully. The other women in the van were covered from head to toe. Scarves around their heads obscured everything but their eyes, which were discreetly focused downward.

"We should have worn something on our heads," I whispered to Stacy. She nodded, cowering in her seat.

At the station, we settled upon an auto-ricksha driver with kind eyes (Stacy was big on kind eyes), and began the final leg to Pat's. The ricksha turned up a long, winding driveway, and stopped at a gate through which we could see several large cement buildings.

A man wearing a turban opened the gate, his eyes registering his disapproval. He grudgingly waved for some boys nearby to unload our luggage, and marched off in the direction of a house, managing to keep several paces ahead of us at all times.

Pat ran out and hugged us. Thanking the man, who was obviously relieved to be done with us, she took us inside.

Pat was still the same. Her brown eyes radiated energy as she fired one question after another. She abruptly stopped talking and scrutinized us.

"We have to do something about your clothes."

"What's wrong with our clothes?" Stacy asked. "These are the most modest things we own."

"You're probably okay for Karachi or some of the big cities, but this is a small town. Western clothes are a 'no-no.' You'll have to wear a *shalwar* chemise. I've got plenty of them, and one size fits all."

We each picked three of the loose tunics which were worn over pants with drawstring waists. They were not in the least flattering. Pat pulled out some long scarves that matched our chemises.

"These are *dupattas*. You have to wear them whenever you leave the house or when someone comes to visit. When you're away from home, they're draped over your head and chest. At home, you just place them across your chest and let the ends fall loosely over your shoulders. Not wearing a *dupatta* is like not wearing a bra. In fact, Pakistani 'women libbers' burn them instead of bras."

Pat took us on a tour of the compound. As we walked down the path, we passed the man who'd led us to her house. This time, he had a smile of approval on his face.

The next day, Pat offered to take us to a bazaar, where everything from clothes to food was sold.

"Before we go," she began, "I need to tell you something. In this culture, women don't go out much, so when they do, they need to take certain precautions.

"It's always assumed that a man's only motivation for speaking to a woman is to seduce her. Therefore, the only men a woman is allowed to speak to are family members or trusted friends. The sexes are strictly segregated to enforce monogamy.

"Even with all the restrictions, Muslim men are very aggressive. Be careful when you're walking through the markets to keep at arm's length from them. If you don't, they'll pinch your behind. Slap them if they do, or they'll think you like it, and they'll do it again."

"What arrogance!" I said. "How can you put up with that?"

"It's not easy. One day when Paul and I were engaged, a man pinched me, and I got so angry that I almost called off the wedding. Since Paul grew up here and considers this home, I knew if I married him, it probably meant living in Pakistan for the rest of my life. I loved Paul, but I didn't think I could ever love Pakistan.

"One more thing: never make eye contact with a man, or he'll think you're flirting."

I practiced scowling. Going to the bazaar didn't sound

like fun anymore. All the way to the market, I had to keep readjusting my *dupatta*. It was made of slippery material, and slid off every few steps. With each readjustment, I fumed about men whose inability to control themselves made such cumbersome attire necessary.

Once at the bazaar, I understood why Pat had warned us. There were few women in the crowds lining the dark, winding alleyways. Men stood in groups, eyeing us. I stiffened my shoulders and clenched my fists until the knuckles turned white.

The bazaars were fascinating. Men dyed the hated *dupattas* (or "dupes," as we had nicknamed them) in vats of boiling water over wood fires on the sidewalk. The scent of exotic perfumes covered the smell of the burning wood. Salesmen unraveled bolts of cloth with a flick of the wrist, trying to tempt us to buy some. Vendors sold kebabs and seasoned nuts. We began to enjoy ourselves.

Having passed through the gauntlet unscathed, I felt cocky. Before I knew what hit me, a motorcycle rider goosed me and raced away. He turned around to make another pass, but this time I was ready. As he reached out to pinch me, I dealt him a resounding blow.

No wonder women didn't go out much.

That night we dined on *chapatis* (flat round breads) and lentil curry, and sipped *chai* (tea made with boiled milk and water). Paul left immediately after dinner to hold a Bible study in one of the dorms. We heard a knock on the door, and I rose to answer it.

"Don't," Pat stopped me. "It's not proper for a woman to answer the door. Since Paul's not here, we have to ignore it."

"But won't they be mad if they find out later that you were home?" Stacy asked.

"No. They'd be embarrassed if I answered the door without Paul here."

Pat said that she and Paul had been asked by a pastor friend to deliver the Easter messages to nine of his congregations in nine different towns. It would take all day.

"Since you'll be here, why don't you join us? The four of us can take turns preaching. We'll spend a few nights with Padre Daniel, and a few with another family.

"Hospitality here is quite different from the United States. Even the shortest visits always last for two or three hours. Also, regular visitation of friends and family is a social obligation. One time, when we hadn't seen a friend in Lahore for awhile, she was so miffed that when we did go see her, she made us stay the whole weekend.

"Guests are king for the duration of their stay. The flip side is that you can't leave until your host says you can."

I noticed that while we were talking, my dupe had slipped into my tea. I could understand what led women to burn them.

Easter morning began at 3:30. We were all staying at Padre Daniel's, and I was sharing a bed in the kitchen with the grandmother.

I pulled on my clothes. For once, I was thankful for my *dupatta*. It covered my greasy hair, which I hadn't been able to shampoo since the beginning of our Easter trip. No one had mentioned showers, and I didn't want to violate some unwritten protocol by asking about one. As we sipped sugary instant coffee, I heard the sound of drums moving closer and closer. Padre Daniel, a tall, stocky man with peppery hair, handed the four of us candles.

"Easter always begins with a predawn candlelight procession through the Christian part of town to the church. Fall in behind the others."

At the church, a celebration of chanting, drum banging, and singing had already begun. Padre Daniel introduced Paul, Pat, Stacy, and me, and Paul preached the first sermon of the day. He seemed to speak Urdu effortlessly.

Daniel had hired a Muslim driver to transport us between the villages in a pickup truck. Inside the covered back were two long wooden benches. We piled in with five other people who were accompanying us for the day.

As we drove, I reviewed the sermon I had prepared. Each of us had struggled with our sermons, trying to find something new and profound to say about Easter. We each had finally come up with theologically intricate pieces that met our satisfaction.

The truck careened—another near miss! I wondered how the driver could stay on the road at such speeds. Our "chauffeur" had celebrated the Muslim sabbath on Friday, and I wondered if he drove this way because we were Christians, or if he was just reckless.

"Where's the church?" I asked, when we finally stopped in a tiny village. All I could see were houses made of grayish dried mud with flat roofs. Stairs leading to the roof clung to the outside of each house like brown spiders.

Pat pointed to a tiny mud building. Inside were five long wooden benches. "Padre Daniel sent one of the children to tell everyone it's time for church."

Before long, a crowd gathered. Many brought mats so they could sit on the floor. We were led to the front, where we sat facing the congregation. A young boy brought us each a bottle of soda to sip during the service.

At last it was time to begin. We were introduced, and some of the children came forward and sang a welcome song. They threw brightly colored pieces of confetti at us, and presented us with bouquets of wild flowers.

Pat gave the sermon in English, then Paul translated it. I noticed that she wasn't giving the elaborate sermon she'd prepared. It was a simple presentation of the Gospel.

On the way to the next service, Pat explained why she'd changed her message. "Most of those people were 'born Christians.' It's a cultural thing. Very few of them understand the message of Christianity."

I began reworking my sermon in my mind.

———————

Each service followed a similar pattern. Pushing and prodding, Daniel kept us on schedule.

In the late afternoon, we stopped at a village where our welcome was not very warm. The service was to take place in a small backyard enclosed by a high wooden fence. Daniel went to gather the people.

As they assembled, I had an uneasy feeling. Most of them were men, and many of them stared at Stacy and me with more relish than seemed proper. Stacy looked nervous. It was her turn to preach.

Bravely, she wrapped her *dupatta* tightly around her head, shrugged her shoulders, and began her sermon. The hostility was evident. Several houses away, curious onlookers stood on their roofs to watch. Some children tried to sneak in the gate, only to be rudely turned away. As Stacy spoke, her *dupatta* slipped bit by bit until the top of her head was exposed, drawing angry stares.

Mercifully, the service was short. When we were back in the truck, I asked Pat what was going on.

"Those people on the rooftops were Muslim and just curious. The children were Muslim, too."

"Why didn't the Christians let them in? It would have been a perfect opportunity for them to hear the Gospel."

"I know," Pat lamented. "But the Christians have been so persecuted by the Muslims in this country that many Christians hate them. I know churches that have actually turned away Muslims who have tried to convert.

"However, there are still Christians who risk their lives to share about Jesus among the Muslims. It's against the law for a Christian to preach to a Muslim."

We didn't finish our rounds until 7:30 p.m. Exhausted, we returned to the house for a light dinner. As we ate, the conversation suddenly became animated. Pat whispered that Daniel was insisting we stay the night, even though we'd promised another family we'd stay with them.

Paul and Daniel discussed the matter at great length, until we were at last able to leave with his blessing. As we were departing, neighbors gathered to watch us go, chattering wildly among themselves.

"They think we had an argument with Daniel," Pat said. "No proper host would let his guest leave so late in the evening unless something were wrong."

———————

At the next pastor's house, where we'd arranged to spend two days, the entire family came out to greet us. Esther, the pastor's daughter, had become one of Pat's good friends. Esther was chunky by American standards, but perfect by Pakistani ones. (Pat said that before she and Paul were married, some of Paul's Pakistani friends had tried to discourage him from marrying her, because they said she was too thin to work in the fields.) Esther was the only one in the family who spoke any English.

The four of us were very tired, and excused ourselves as soon as it was polite to do so. We were to sleep in a small room detached from the main house that contained two double beds. Although this arrangement wouldn't be considered proper in the States, housing shortages in this area made it a common practice.

We stayed dressed since we'd be sharing the room with Paul, but we removed the baggy pants. Modesty wasn't a question, since our long tunics covered our knees. (Men also wear *shalwar* chemises, though not as fancy as the women's.)

Stacy and I had just taken off our baggy pants when there was a knock at the door.

"Quick, jump in bed," Pat yelled. "It's offensive to show your legs, even to members of the same sex."

We scrambled under the covers as Paul, the only one who hadn't gotten ready for bed yet, answered the door. It was one of the pastor's sons, checking to see if the fan worked. He tinkered with it for a few minutes, then left.

I'd just begun to relax when there was another knock. Again, we jumped under the covers. It was Esther. She set down a pitcher of water on the nightstand and said goodnight. A few minutes later, there was another knock and another scramble. This time it was Esther's mother.

"Do you have enough blankets?" Once we reassured her that we were comfortable, she left. (We laughed, because just a few minutes earlier, they had been concerned about whether the fan was keeping us cool enough.)

We turned off the light and tried to fall asleep. Another knock. Paul dressed quickly and opened the door. Esther handed him a mosquito coil to keep the mosquitoes away.

After several more visits, we were left alone. We all collapsed into a fit of giggles, which we fought to suppress lest anyone come out to see what the noise was all about.

The next day, Pat and Paul set off to visit several families right after breakfast. Stacy and I opted to stay behind, hoping for some quiet time; we were tired of trying to keep up a conversation with people who knew only a few words of English.

Esther knocked at our door. Apparently, it was rude to leave guests unattended for even a moment.

"Do you like chicken?" she asked.

Since it seemed like a harmless question, I innocently replied, "Yes, I like chicken a lot."

A few minutes later, we heard a chicken squawking in the courtyard. We realized that it was about to be sacrificed for our pleasure.

Esther's brother came in looking dejected. The chicken had escaped. I secretly cheered for the chicken, though as a city girl, I had a morbid curiosity about how a chicken is prepared from scratch.

The brother soon renewed the chase with vigor. He summoned Stacy and me to watch the death blow. I hung back, scrunching my eyes shut. Stacy, on the other hand,

walked right up to the cement block where he was bran-
dishing a large carving knife. He graciously offered Stacy
the honor of killing the chicken. She looked tempted, then
declined. Esther's brother deftly slit the chicken's throat
and began ripping feathers and skin off in big chunks.

Now Esther took over. She wielded the knife without
regard for leg, breast, or thigh. Once hacked into indeci-
pherable little bits, it was thrown into a pot with chunks
of garlic and onions. Alas, I had hoped in vain for some
good old fried chicken.

Then Esther and her brother discussed where to cook
the chicken.

"How about the kitchen?" I suggested.

"No, my mother's using it," Esther said.

I peeked inside the kitchen anyway. When I saw it, I
could understand the problem. There was barely enough
space for one person to work. The kitchen was separate
from the house, and was about the size of an average
American closet. The floor was hard, packed dirt. At one
end, a small wood fire was blazing. There was no electricity. If they needed light, they used kerosene lamps.

Esther motioned for us to follow her. She proudly
pulled out a never-before-used pressure cooker from the
dining room. She handed it to me. Although adept at things
like microwaves and food processors, I had no idea about
the workings of a pressure cooker. I remembered hearing
when I was a little girl that one of my relatives had made
a minor mistake when releasing the steam. It exploded in
her face and left her with severe burns. I shook my head.

"Look at the directions," Stacy brightly suggested.

They were in Japanese.

We decided to give it a try anyway. The moment of
truth came half an hour later. The pressure had mounted
both in the room and in the cooker. The chicken must
surely be done. Esther and her mother backed away. I
inched toward the pot and gingerly released the steam.

When the hissing stopped, I eased off the cover. There were smiles all around.

Hours had now passed since Esther first brought up the subject of chicken, and I was famished. Esther and her mother hovered over us and insisted that we keep eating until we couldn't force down another bite. Then they brought out dessert: a pinkish gelatin garnished with raisins and coconut shavings. It was after 4:00 p.m. when we finished lunch, and washing dishes took another hour. We had spent almost an entire day preparing and eating one meal. And this was a typical day for a Pakistani woman.

There was still no sign of Pat and Paul, who had been due back hours ago. It was pouring rain, and we should have already left for Gujranwala. Pat had language classes early the next morning.

Two more hours passed. Then they burst in, laden down with material and *shalwar* chemises. Pat said that it was a tradition to give clothes to new brides when they came to visit. They'd gone to see every family they knew in town, in order not to offend anyone.

Because of the lateness of the hour and the rain, Esther's family now decided we'd have to spend another night there. Negotiations had to be worked out, all parties being careful not to offend. A mutually satisfactory agreement was reached. We could leave that evening, but only after we ate something.

I groaned. I was still full from lunch. But it was getting late, and the weather was getting worse. The longer we waited, the more impassable the roads would be. We ate as quickly as was polite, and two hours later, were on our way. At least we thought we were.

We were climbing into two auto-rickshas to take us to the bus station when Esther's father ran out and began speaking to Paul in rapid-fire Urdu.

"He insists that one of his sons accompany you to the bus station," Paul said. "They're a conservative family, and feel that two women shouldn't travel alone in a ricksha—the driver might run off with you." From what I had observed since we'd arrived, it didn't seem improbable.

By now, I really wished we could have stayed another night. The rain was fierce. When we arrived at the station and all the passengers were seated in our minivan, the driver proceeded to take down everyone's name, address, and passport number.

We were facing five hours on a treacherous road, and were being delayed by some silly paperwork. I was totally exasperated.

"Last night, a bus crashed on this road, and all the passengers were killed," Paul said. "Because they hadn't compiled a passenger list, it'll be impossible to identify the charred remains."

It hadn't even rained last night! I gathered my *dupatta* around me, this time more for comfort than conformity. It was going to be a long night.

16

Where East Meets West (Nanci)

"I've got a great idea. Let's join a truck caravan."

Stacy and I were discussing the best way to get to Israel. Our around-the-world airline ticket didn't cover this leg of the journey.

"You've got to be kidding," Stacy grimaced. "Getting to the Middle East from Pakistan is not like driving from New York to California. There are a few minor obstacles in the way—like Iran and Iraq."

Adventure companies offered overland transportation to the Middle East, and it all sounded pretty exciting to me. Who wouldn't want to follow ancient trade routes that linked Asia to Europe? "Well, I suppose it would be hard to get transit visas for those countries anyway," I conceded. "Maybe we can go to Lebanon instead."

Stacy took off her dupe and pretended to wring my neck. "A rupee for your thoughts," she said.

"Believe it or not, I'm gonna miss being in developing nations. Even Pakistan. It's been exciting to have to trust God for everything—especially our health and safety. Now it'll be too easy to start relying on ourselves again."

Pat came in the room. "I'll miss you guys. Marriage is wonderful, but I get so lonely for girlfriends. It's one of the occupational hazards of being a missionary."

She handed Stacy a jar of peanut butter.

"Ramadan starts tomorrow, and you'll need something to snack on. Most restaurants are closed during the day. I try to sneak a sandwich in a bathroom somewhere. I don't know what Jordan is like, but in Pakistan, Muslims are offended if you eat in front of them during their fast days."

Ramadan is the month Muslims set aside to fast as part of their religious duty. It takes place during the ninth month of the Islamic year, based on a lunar calendar in which each month begins with a new moon. During this time, every able-bodied adult is expected to abstain from eating or drinking from dawn to sunset. Only the elderly, the very young, and the infirm are excused.

"How long will it take you to get to Israel?" Pat asked.

"About five days. We overnight in the United Arab Emirates, then fly to Jordan early the next morning. Once in Jordan, it should take about three days to get our passes for the West Bank," Stacy said.

"Weren't they expecting you in Israel today?"

"We tried to telephone the guest house in Haifa where we'll be working to let them know we'll be late. But there's not a direct line from Pakistan to Israel."

Pat laughed. "I wouldn't think so."

Friends from our church in Virginia were the directors of Stella Carmel, a guest house affiliated with an Episcopal organization. When I had told them about our trip, they had invited us to come work with them for a month.

"That reminds me, Stacy, did you get a new passport?" Pat asked.

"No. I'm gonna take a chance that the Jordanian officials won't see the Israeli stamp in mine. But if something goes wrong, I'll see you in a few days."

I tried to laugh it off. As much as Stacy loved crossing "Things To Do" off her list, she loved beating the odds even more. She had stubbornly refused to get a new passport, even though she knew Arab countries have a law forbidding anyone with an Israeli stamp in their passport to enter their country. Not only did Stacy have an Israeli stamp, but her passport had been issued in Tel Aviv when her other one was stolen on a visit there years ago.

When we reached the United Arab Emirates, we couldn't wait to check into a modern hotel, our first chance in three months. Instead, we spent the night on a bench in the airport. A travel agent in Nepal had failed to tell us that hotels in the U.A.E. were off limits to unescorted females.

Then we discovered that our luggage was lost. And if that weren't enough, the lost baggage official laughed at the Pakistani clothes we had on!

We'd been especially careful to dress very modestly. But for some strange reason, it was all right for women in the U.A.E. to wear Western clothes, but not all right for them to stay alone in a hotel room. And I'd thought life was going to be easier when we left developing nations.

Our short stay in the U.A.E. was difficult, but we knew that the Jordanian border could be much worse.

"You go through first. Whenever I go first, I get stopped," Stacy whispered to me as we stood in the visa line at the Jordanian airport the next day.

"It's my freckles. Have you ever met a dishonest person with freckles?" I said. I made my way up to the long wooden counter. The customs official quickly leafed through my passport, stamped it, and motioned me on to the baggage claim area. Instead, I lingered behind to watch as he began thumbing through Stacy's.

When the stamp came down on her passport, I began to breathe. But not for long. For some reason he started thumbing through the passport again, slowly examining each page. Stacy looked over at me, helpless. The official called two co-workers over and handed the passport to each of them. They conferred in Arabic. Then he took a red pen and wrote "Canceled" across the visa he'd just issued to Stacy.

Well, Stacy, I thought. *Your luck just ran out.*

"But you can't do this," Stacy stammered. "I don't have enough money to fly back to Pakistan." Tears welled in her eyes and her voice quivered. By now Stacy had lost all chutzpah.

While we stood there, we saw two people ceremonially ushered to the deportation lounge.

Another official approached us, and he showed no interest as Stacy argued her case. He dismissed her with an abrupt wave of his hand and motioned to the next person in line. Stacy stayed right where she was. I held my breath. After what seemed like an eternity, a different official, annoyed that Stacy was in everyone's way, walked over.

"Why are you still here?" he demanded.

"I've got to have a visa," Stacy pleaded. She began telling her story again, and by this time, she was sobbing. He cut her off in mid-sentence, threw up his hands, and motioned for her to follow him into an office.

I sat outside and prayed feverishly. Half an hour later, Stacy walked by me and waved her passport.

"We're free to go," she said beaming, "on the condition that I go to the American Embassy first thing in the morning and get a new passport.

"He was worried about separating us. He said it's not good for a woman to travel alone." For once, Muslim chauvinism worked in our favor. And when we left the customs area, another prayer was answered. Two lone dusty bags circled on the carousel.

Once in Jordan, Stacy got a new passport at the American Embassy, then we dropped off our passports at the Jordanian government office in charge of granting permits to cross the King Hussein Bridge into Israel, or the part better known to both sides as the "West Bank." We kept waiting for our permits, but after a week, decided to follow through ourselves.

It's amazing how government buildings look alike all

over the world. After wandering through a maze of corridors, we found the office we were looking for. Outside the door was a water fountain between two benches.

"Nanci, I'm feeling dizzy again," Stacy said, leaning against the wall. "I'll sit here while you check on our passes." Her hypoglycemia was back.

The clerk dumped out a box of multi-colored passports. "No Sells. No Hogan," he said matter-of-factly.

It was my turn to be assertive. "What do you mean they're not there? We've been waiting a week. Last time I came, you told me it would only take three days."

"Lady, it's Ramadan." When I didn't budge, he finally said, "There's one more place I can check."

While I waited, there was a commotion in the hall. I peeked out the door to see an irate official storm up to the water fountain and unplug it.

"What happened?" I asked Stacy.

"Well, I was thirsty. The first time I got a drink, people just stared at me. I didn't think anything of it. I'd just started to get another drink when this man came running out of an office and unplugged the water fountain. I forgot that Muslims don't even drink water during fasting hours."

In the middle of the commotion, the clerk reappeared and slapped two passes in my hand—our permits to cross the Jordan River.

"This is the King Hussein Bridge?" I exclaimed as our bus lumbered across a bridge about ten feet wide and no more than twenty feet long.

"I can't believe we had to wait a week for a pass for this thing," Stacy protested. "We could have just walked across." The bus stopped in front of a large building.

"This is the Israeli border," the driver announced. "You have to check all your luggage through Israeli customs before you can go any further." We went, grabbed our bags, and found the right line.

We waited and waited. We'd been standing in line over a hour, and the guard was interrogating a slight, red-haired woman in front of us at great length.

"Stacy, try to hear what he's saying," I whispered, knowing what a skilled eavesdropper she was.

"She has an American passport, but was born in Syria. The guard is asking her if she has any connections with the PLO or any other terrorist organization. She said she hasn't been to an Arab country since she immigrated to the United States 20 years ago. She's come to visit some family in Israel."

"She looks harmless enough to me," I murmured. "I say let her in."

The official was now going through every item in her luggage. Then he took the empty bags to be X-rayed. Even though he found nothing suspicious, he refused to let her in the country. He forced her to return to Jordan. I'd expected relations between the Israelis and Arabs to be tense; however, I was surprised at the extent it was played out by customs officials on both sides of the border.

After talking to several bus drivers, we found out that there were no direct routes to Haifa, even though we weren't far from the town. We had no choice but to go to Jerusalem and get a connecting bus. Getting from Pakistan to Stella Carmel hadn't been as exciting as my idea of joining a truck caravan had sounded, but it had been far from uneventful.

Stacy flagged down a taxi once we hit Haifa. We flipped a coin to see whose turn it was to negotiate. "How much?" I inquired.

"Thirty shekels."

"Too much. How about 20."

"Take it or leave it, lady." He started to drive away. I ran after him. By this time, all I wanted was a hot shower and a bed.

I waited for him to load our luggage into the trunk. He

sat tapping his fingers on the steering wheel. Finally Stacy said, "I think we're supposed to handle our own bags."

We heaved our belongings into the back seat and crawled in beside them.

"Pay me now," he said.

I whipped out my wallet, counted out the money, and flung it on the seat beside him.

"I can tell I'm going to love this country," I hissed to Stacy. "I hope everyone's as nice as this guy."

The blue of the Mediterranean soothed my nerves as we climbed the cedar-covered mountains high above the port city. "Well, we're back in the West," Stacy observed, and sniffed the fresh air.

The taxi came to a stop at the end of a long driveway. "You can get out," the driver said. He waited barely long enough for us to wrestle our luggage out before doing a U-turn and racing back down the road for another fare.

Our friend, the director, came running to greet us.

"We were really worried. We expected you days ago."

We followed him into the lounge of a large, two-story, white building. "Stella is a conference and retreat center for both local and international groups. You'll be working with other volunteers who help run the place."

He handed us an orientation packet and showed us to our rooms. I unpacked and showered, then began reading the material. Laughing, I called Stacy into my room.

"Listen to this," I read: "'Avoid any eye contact with members of the opposite sex, as it will likely be understood as a sexual advance. Girls should always have their shoulders covered. Shorts and short skirts are forbidden....Friendships between young people of the opposite sex are not acceptable....It is considered impolite to refuse hospitality....It can give offense if a visit is too short and rushed....' Sound familiar?"

The director's wife knocked at the door. "Here's some mail for you. We've been holding it for a long time." We tore open the packages and were amazed by the number of letters that tumbled out. Our Christmas mail had caught up with us. And to think we were ready to pack it in three months earlier in Singapore. Now we realized even more how dependent we were on others. We sat down and basked in their long-awaited words of encouragement.

A Holy Detente (Nanci)

Stacy came into my room, and I could tell immediately that she had some mischief in mind.

"Everyone around here's too serious. I think we should do something to lighten them up," she announced, plopping onto my bed.

I had to ask, "Well, what do you think we should do?"

"Remember those Arab headdresses we bought in Jordan? I think we should wear them to breakfast."

When the other volunteers saw us, they laughed. But Katie, the Irish housekeeper, ran over to our table.

"Girls, what are you doing?" Her lilting voice rose a couple of octaves.

"We have a group of Arab Christians here this morning, and they might think you're making fun of them by wearing the headdresses. It's a good thing they're not black or checkered. The PLO wear those, and our Jewish guests would have been very upset.

"I know you meant well. But in this country there's so much tension that even a seemingly harmless joke can have serious political implications."

We meekly took off the *keffiyehs*. We hadn't realized how much the Arab-Israeli conflict affected every aspect of life here. But if anyone could anticipate an explosive situation, it was Katie. She was from Northern Ireland.

Walking through the *souk* in Old Jerusalem made me

uneasy. Where only yesterday Arab shopkeepers had noisily touted their wares, now there was a deadly quiet. The shopkeepers had declared another strike to protest the Israeli occupation of the West Bank.

After working at Stella for a month, we'd decided to explore Israel and see how the Gospel was being preached in the land of its origin. I also wanted to get a better understanding of the political situation.

Sirens shattered the uneasy calm, and police rushed to cordon off the road in front of us. I asked an onlooker what was happening.

"Someone left a package on the road. It could be a bomb," he said matter-of-factly.

I'd seen signs reminding people to report unattended packages, but I didn't realize how quickly such reports were acted upon. The bomb squad cautiously approached the package.

"Does this happen often?" I asked.

"Yes. They have to inspect every package that's reported. Some of them are really bombs. They go off, killing whoever's around."

Before long, the all-clear signal sounded, and things returned to normal. It was a false alarm—this time. I questioned one of the policemen at the blockade.

"It's part of the *intifada*," he said. "The Palestinians want the West Bank and the Gaza Strip back. This has been going on since December of 1987.

I thought back on what we'd learned about the *intifada*. In December, 1987, a mass movement began with an uprising of the residents of the West Bank and the Gaza Strip. For the first time, PLO factions worked under a unified leadership, and various Muslim groups started working together, all to establish a Palestinian nation.

The officer continued, "Palestinian children are taught from birth to hate the Israelis, and even a small child who participates in the *intifada* is considered a hero. We've got

our work cut out just trying to maintain peace and order."
I remembered a conversation I'd had with a man in Jordan while Stacy was at the U.S. Embassy applying for a new passport. I'd ducked into a hotel for a snack, since hotels were the only place food might be available during Ramadan. I saw a familiar face in the lobby, and recognized him as a Jordanian exchange student I had met in graduate school.

He told me that he now worked for the Jordanian Ministry of Information. We began discussing Arab-Israeli relations. He said that the Israelis manipulated the media to make the *intifada* seem worse than it was, in order to justify their use of force. He cited several recent incidents which were reported quite differently on Israeli and Jordanian television.

"The Palestinians on the occupied West Bank are exploited terribly," he told me. "Over 100,000 of them commute to Israel to do menial work that the Israelis refuse to do. Since they're there illegally, they're not protected by Israel's labor laws."

Now, remembering that conversation, I asked the Israeli policeman, "Don't the Palestinians have a right to their own homeland?" I asked.

"When the U.N. partitioned Palestine in 1948, they set aside land for a Palestinian homeland. The Palestinians rejected it, saying that having no land was better than having only part of the land they were entitled to. We didn't ask for the West Bank. We won it during the Six Days War in 1967."

It was hard to know whom to believe. My Jordanian friend and the Israeli policeman had one interesting thing in common: both were both reasonable and well-informed.

"Nanci," Stacy said one morning, "let's go to Bethlehem. According to the paper, there's fighting there every morning, and you've wanted to see the action firsthand."

Now that the opportunity was actually here, I wasn't so anxious to put myself under fire.

"Supposedly, the Arabs don't throw rocks at tourists," Stacy reassured me. We decided to take the risk.

The Arab buses in Old Jerusalem that went to the West Bank were on strike, so we decided to take an Arab *sharut,* a shared taxi. Fortunately, many others wanted to go to Bethlehem that day, so our taxi filled quickly and we left.

Twenty minutes later, we were there. The town was filled with tour buses and souvenir stands.

"Are you nervous?" Stacy asked.

"No. If it were too dangerous, all these tour buses wouldn't be here."

We visited the tourist spots, all the while straining to catch a glimpse of a confrontation. We stalled as long as we could at the church commemorating the place where Christ was born. Then we strolled the streets—slowly. Disappointed, we headed back for Jerusalem.

Later that afternoon, we learned that there had been a huge altercation in Bethlehem that day. Right where we'd been. Right after we'd left.

We kept meeting people at Stella Carmel who were victims of the Holocaust. One of them was a middle-aged French Jew who was there to write a book about her life. She only left her room for meals.

Although she had been protected by a Christian family, and was never sent to a concentration camp, the Holocaust was the formative experience of her life. Past and future had no meaning except as it related to it.

One evening, Stacy and I happened to sit at her table for dinner. Two hours later, she was still telling us stories of how it had ravaged her life. It had happened 45 years earlier. It made me shudder to think about the potential legacy the current Arab-Israeli conflict would have in a country where children on both sides were taught hatred the minute they were born.

Another lady we met, a German, described growing up in an anti-Semitic village during World War II. "My family actually turned people over to the Nazis. I'm still guilt-ridden by what they did. That's why I'm here. I want to try to make it up to the Jews."

I began thinking about Corrie ten Boom, a Dutch woman who at mid-life was incarcerated in a German concentration camp for hiding Jews from the Nazis. Both her sister and her father died in the camps. She later became a famous evangelist and writer.

One evening, years after her release, a man came up to speak with her after one of her talks. She recognized him immediately as one of the more brutal guards at her camp.

"Please forgive me," he cried, extending his hand.

For several long seconds, Corrie hesitated. She prayed that God would give her the strength to do what she knew she had to do. She reached out and shook his hand. It was an act of healing, both for him and for her.

The last thing I did before leaving Israel was to visit the Garden Tomb in Jerusalem. It was in a quiet oasis off a busy street. Flowers surrounded it, their bright pinks and blues a perfect contrast to the bald, craggy hillside. I sat on a bench shaded by an olive tree to enjoy the peace.

Several minutes passed before I could bring myself to explore the tomb. Peering inside, I saw that I was alone.

The sight moved me like none other had in all Israel; the tomb's very emptiness was so significant. Too many of the other sights commemorating Jesus' life and ministry were little more than historical landmarks.

The Garden Tomb was different. Even though disputes rage over the exact location of Christ's burial place, I knew that it was not a physical place that we worshiped, but rather a risen Christ. The longer I stayed inside the tomb, the more I could feel His presence.

18

Pass the Plaster (Stacy)

Thoughts of spackle, sandpaper, and primer danced in my head, and I couldn't remember which came first. Our assignment: to paint the halls—walls, baseboards, and trim of a YWAM building in Amsterdam. What had started out as fun and novel now had become boring, hard work. So this was what it meant to be a "mission builder."

Rather than conduct interviews about the work taking place in Holland, we agreed to offer our services for a month toward the renovation of a five-story building in Amsterdam, where 150 missionaries from around the world were housed, fed, and trained. In return for laboring 40 hours a week, we received room and board.

Our first day at work, Ruud, our Dutch foreman, meticulously explained our assignment. He was obviously a person concerned with tremendous detail. I am not. I could see great potential for problems.

Nanci and I plunged into our work with diligence and cautious optimism. We showed up in the appropriate attire each morning: T-shirts and old shorts. We equipped ourselves with the proper apparatus: gloves, putty knives, spackle, sandpaper, and tarps. At least we looked the part.

After one week, we had finished one hall.

Ruud came to inspect. Carefully, he ran his fingers over boards that we had puttied, sanded, re-puttied, and painted. Squinting his dark eyes, he knelt down and scrutinized the walls for any runs or splotches. We followed him around, waiting for accolades.

"Not bad," he said softly, and walked away.

I was crushed.

Not bad! I thought. I had poured my heart and soul into this job. Not only were we unpaid, we were unappreciated.

I later learned that the Dutch manner was to avoid being overly gratuitous or complimentary.

"They have difficulty accepting praise, so they don't know how to give it," a fellow volunteer explained. "'Not bad' was Ruud's way of saying you did a great job."

The second week began just like the first. At 6:30 a.m., I was summoned from a deep sleep by my watch's alarm, and pulled on my pink T-shirt (now speckled eggshell white) and blue and white striped knee-length shorts.

Though I usually leapt out of bed, I could barely rise. Even with the weekend of rest, I could no longer put on my shoes while standing up. I slowly lifted one foot at a time to tighten the laces, then pounded on the wall to signal that I was ready. (Nanci's room was next door.)

We hobbled together down four flights of stairs, one painful step at a time, holding to the rails lest a leg give out. The dining hall was in the basement. After breakfast, we limped to an assembly line of tables to make our lunch. By 7:30, we were back in the basement supply room.

"Good morning, ladies," Ruud greeted us cheerfully. We were the only ladies who had signed up for this duty.

A few minutes later, we were joined by a man from Boston, an energetic carpenter who had come with his wife and three children to donate his skills for three months. Right behind him were two shy, native Dutchmen. Our crew was complete, and we were given our assignments.

The intercom kept interrupting our work. "Attention, please. All mission builders report to the loading dock."

Whatever we were doing, we stopped to rush downstairs and unload trucks of food and supplies. It was heavy work, but sometimes we were rewarded with sweets.

At the end of the second week, we had earned a promotion to a more difficult chore: we were given a hallway where brick walls had replaced doorways, and told to disguise them with plaster.

Ruud led us to a closet which contained a bag of gray powder, a metal tub, water buckets, and a machine that resembled a giant eggbeater. Here we were to make the plaster, holding onto a beater which had the size and kick of a jackhammer. I nicknamed the closet "the bakery," and likened our work to baking a cake. Unfortunately, some days our batter was lumpy and our icing ran.

As I labored in the hallways, I often overheard interesting things going on behind closed doors. (I still was not above eavesdropping.) In one room, a team practiced a Christian drama; in another, a group planned a trip to eastern Europe to conduct training seminars for pastors; in another, musicians perfected their acts to be presented in clubs all over Europe. I wanted to be a part of "the action." Mission building was the bottom rung on the ladder of ministries as far as I was concerned.

One day, I saw a young man prop up his grubby feet on a wall we had just painted. I looked at him in horror and bit my lip.

When I got back to my room, I called Nanci. "I don't want to sound superior or anything, but don't you think God has something better for us to do with our time?"

I continued scrubbing the paint off my hands and waited for her answer. It was a look of disapproval.

By the next day, my attitude was better, and I felt I could handle anything. God and Ruud decided to test me.

Six American teenage girls had arrived over the weekend, and we were put in charge of them. It was our job to train, supervise, and "baby-sit" the giggling group, who appeared to have nothing in mind except the opposite sex.

I had always managed to avoid working with teenagers. They made me edgy, to say the least. Our first morning together, I asked one of the girls to run quickly to the supply room and get a trowel I needed right away. Twenty minutes later, she returned, empty-handed. She had run into a cute male volunteer, started talking, and had forgotten what she had gone for. One of the other girls offered to go back with her.

"Never mind," I mumbled. "I'll get it myself."

They complained that the sanding and plastering were ruining their nails (as it had already done ours), and asked if they couldn't do something else. They believed in "quantity over quality," so while Nanci and I painstakingly sanded one door frame, they finished entire corridors.

Lunch breaks always proved a challenge. After 45 minutes of freedom, they came strolling leisurely back, hands hidden in bags of chips, still gabbing about the boys they'd spied on the streets.

By the end of each day, hardened plaster was glued to the floors in globs, and white dust covered everything. Tools, sandpaper, and buckets were randomly strewn about. The sight was more than they could take, so we dismissed them to the showers and tackled the job alone.

Our productivity declined remarkably that week, and our patience was tried on more than one occasion, but by the time it was over, I had a better understanding of teenagers, and I think they felt the same about us.

Toward the end of our stay, Nanci and I returned to our rooms one evening to find two bunches of flowers wrapped in tissue paper and held together with a big red bow. An anonymous note thanked us for "the good job we had done" and the "joyful manner" in which we had done it. We chose to think that we knew from whom it had come.

Two days later, we began the last leg of our journey, a patchwork of flights from Amsterdam to London to Boston to Guatemala to Belize, Central America.

As we left the YWAM center in Amsterdam, I stopped to admire the walls.

19

Our Bonaventure (Stacy)

"You'll be staying in the condos," the YWAM Belize director told us over the phone. In our year of travel, we'd survived an amazing array of accommodations. With only six weeks left, I was delighted to be going out in style.

Belize City, the largest town in a tiny country of barely 200,000 people, made me feel like I was back in the rural South of my childhood. Houses stood on stilts along swampy river banks, protected from the frequent floods that assailed them. Buildings were nailed together from a hodgepodge of various colors, sizes, and shapes of wood. The people were black, not Hispanic, as I'd thought they'd be in Central America; spoke Pidgin English; and hid under umbrellas to escape the relentless sun.

I was puzzled. Tucked away in my daypack was a recent *Skin Diver* article that lavished praise on this little-known country, describing it as a premier vacation spot. As far as I could tell, there were no tourists in sight, and the choice of accommodations was dubious.

An hour out of town, we pulled off the "road" onto a thin dirt path, crossed a river on a small boat, climbed up a steep bank, and pushed our way through jungle foliage to a clearing where some old vans were parked.

If ever there was a missionary setting right out of a movie, this was it. I could envision pioneers in pith helmets and khaki jungle gear cutting through the vines with machetes to come greet us. What I wanted to know was: *Where were the condos?*

Two young volunteers arrived and picked up our bags. We followed them through knee-deep grass to where the base director stood, smiling, in front of ten tiny square wooden huts arranged in two rows.

"Welcome to the condos!" he said.

When our hostess brought sheets, towels, and a pitcher of water, I asked if they had an iron. She laughed.

"No need for that. Just hang up your clothes, and in this humidity, they'll be fine by morning."

Sure enough, in a few hours our clothes were wrinkle-free. My blonde hair was also straight as a board and Nanci's was a mass of dark curly ringlets clinging to her head.

YWAMers literally carved the Banana Bank Campus out of the jungle in 1983. Working with machetes six days a week for over a year, they hacked a 50-acre clearing.

The staff of 50, as well as short-term visiting teams, squeeze into condos, small houses, and dorms. Thanks to a new generator, there's now electricity where previously only candles were used. The grounds are graced with wild parrots, toucans, football-sized frogs, snakes, scorpions, two-foot iguanas, and killer bees.

The fastest route back to town was across the river surrounding the camp on three sides. A rope pulled a rusty metal dinghy from one side to the other, and a short walk led to a bus stop serviced sporadically.

Every morning, a cowbell broke the silence at 6:00 a.m. I was already awake; it was difficult to sleep with sheets sticking to my body. I headed straight through the grass to a cement block building, where shower heads were separated by moldy curtains. There was only one knob for water, so obviously there was only one temperature. By the time I finished showering, I was already sweaty again.

A second bell rang at 6:30 to summon everyone to breakfast at the tin-roofed, open-air dining hall. Meals were served family-style from long, wooden picnic tables. Coffee and cold water were passed around along with a jar of white pills.

"Malaria medicine," the woman sitting by me explained the first morning. "Once a week if you're trying to prevent it; triple doses daily when you get it."

I shook one tablet out and passed the jar on.

Our second day, we met with the acting director, Matt, a gentle South African man, and his wife Whitney. He told us that Belize was settled by British pirates who imported black, female slaves to act as servants and lovers. Marriage was not integral to the early culture, and that same attitude still prevails. Today, there are more missionaries per capita in Belize than in any other country. Yet Christianity is still a nominal force in most of its people's lives.

The people are a diverse mix of Creole, Caribbean, Garifuna, Mestizo, Mayan, Indian, Latin refugee, British, and Chinese. (For the equivalent of $10,000, a Hong Kong resident can become a citizen of Belize. In order to get out of Hong Kong before the Chinese takeover in 1997, hundreds have immigrated to Belize, and many have opened restaurants which have become the country's best.) Despite the vast ethnic mixture, Caribbean culture prevails.

YWAM teams work in refugee settlements, assist in Belize's one hospital, train local church leaders, work with youth groups, and oversee small farm projects. They have also established a crisis pregnancy and counseling center.

Nanci and I pitched into work by reorganizing the campus library. Then we were assigned to the office, a pleasant assignment, since this was the only air-conditioned building for miles around.

There wasn't much work for us to do. It was late summer, which meant a steady influx of teams from the United States. I began feeling lost and bored in the crowd. The wear and tear of travel had begun taking its toll. We'd been moving usually every three days for more than a year.

I also worried about the plague that was moving through camp. Some mysterious illness had struck without warning. Each day, the breakfast talk centered around who had fallen prey to it the day before. Throughout the night, we heard the swift rustling of grass as some new victim rushed past our condo to the outhouse. Nanci and I reassured ourselves that we had remained virtually unscathed thus far, and undoubtedly had tough immune systems.

Ten days after our arrival, it hit me. I recognized the aches, low energy, and stomach disorders that signaled its onset. I lay in a hammock, alternating between shivering chills and feverish sweats.

For ten days, I was unable to keep food down. My name was posted on the sick list each morning. Plastic pitchers in a community refrigerator had the names of the ailing penciled on them. They contained rehydration fluids that were essential to replenish our bodily fluids daily.

As a birthday surprise, Nanci had made plans for us to visit one of the outer cays for a weekend of snorkeling. I was feeling well enough to walk around by now, and we were sure that meant a rapid recovery. With her help, I made my way across the river and up to the road to wait for the bus to Belize City. Nanci carried both our bags, and I reassured her from time to time by muttering, "I'm feeling better. I'm feeling better."

I sat by a window on the bus to town. The 70-minute ride was the worst experience of our entire trip. I struggled to remain conscious by counting off each mile marker we rattled past. My tongue felt like parchment. The voices of other passengers floated around me dimly. Nanci said not a word, nor did she need to. We both knew this was serious.

When the bus reached town, I stumbled down the steps and collapsed, delirious, on the sidewalk. Nanci panicked. I needed help in a hurry. She knew there was only one hospital in the country, and she had no idea which city it was in.

While I had been confined to my bed at the base a few days earlier, Nanci had worked at a place in town. She remembered that it was near the bus station, and there had been a volunteer doctor on duty that day. With no time to waste, she flagged down a taxi to take us there—to the pregnancy crisis center!

For three hours, I lay on a hard wooden bench inside the church YWAM leased for their clinic. My body shook violently. My temperature soared to 104.

People gathered around to pray for my recovery. They also prayed that I didn't have the malaria my symptoms indicated. When the fever went down enough that I was coherent, I was helped to a taxi. Much too sick to attempt the bus ride back to campus, we checked into the only Western hotel in town. Days later, I emerged from the hotel room. Miraculously, I had survived.

Back at the base that night, we were awakened by shrill screams coming from the women's dorm and our neighboring condos shortly before dawn. I decided it was probably a scorpion, spider, or snake—nothing unusual—and I could wait until breakfast to find out which.

It turned out that it was the annual onslaught of marching ants. Once a year, they showed up at the camp, thousands of them in a straight line which could neither be stopped nor redirected. That year, the path they chose was right through the middle of the women's dorm and two condos. They marched over beds, across bodies, and through sheets, clothes, and whatever else lay in their path, leaving stinging bites in their wake.

Two days after returning from my birthday fiasco, we were asked to assist a Canadian medical team going to a remote area of southern Belize. They were volunteering their services in Ruland and Lynn Rasmussen's community. I wondered how anything could be more remote than where we were. I wasn't fully recovered, but we'd be with doctors and nurses if anything went wrong.

Belize's unpaved Hummingbird Highway is notorious for causing the demise of vehicles. Ours succumbed just about sunset, with 13 of us cramped in a covered pickup full of boxes of medical gear and medications. The alternatives were to sleep by the side of the road, or pray that a bus would pass by and take one of us into town for help. We piled out of the truck and started praying. I decided to walk a little way down the road.

"I wouldn't go that way," one of the doctors quietly advised me. "There's a cobra in the middle of the road."

I needed no further warning, and returned to the safety of the truck, away from snakes, mountain lions, and blue-eyed tarantulas.

Eventually, a bus came by, and ten of us got on, leaving three men to guard the supplies. We promised to send help in the morning. Two hours later, we arrived in the town of Dangriga and made our way to a missionary's home.

At daylight, we heard the sputtering and clunking of a vehicle outside. A Swiss family of mechanics, out for an evening hike, had run across our little band and put them up for the night. They were even able to repair the truck enough for it to make it to Dangriga. The truck hung on to life until we were in sight of the Rasmussen's house, where the transmission gave one final lurch and died forever. We gathered our gear and walked the last quarter mile.

Ruland and Lynn's airy, two-story home stood on stilts in a clearing two miles off a dirt road. There was no electricity or potable water. All supplies were either brought in from a town an hour away or harvested in the jungle. During the rainy season, the Rasmussens were even more isolated when the land flooded. Mountain lions roamed the vicinity, and a boa constrictor had killed the family chicken the week before. Scorpions fell from rafters to beds, and mosquitoes devoured those who hadn't thoroughly doused themselves in bug repellent. Only the hardiest of missionaries applied for this post.

We were at a pretty low point by this time. Tired, hot, hungry, stranded, and a day behind in our clinic work, we struggled to be optimistic. There was one reason to hope: Bobby had arrived before us.

Bobby was a servant to fellow missionaries. An auto mechanic by trade, he had learned to repair almost anything. Missionaries in this part of Belize were frequently hampered by broken equipment. When Bobby wasn't pastoring his church in the far southern town of Punta Gorda, he was busy repairing things.

The day before we arrived, he had a sense that there was trouble at Ruland's. He drove for more than four hours over nearly impassable roads to offer assistance. When we came walking up to the house carrying all our belongings, he knew he had been sent. He spent that afternoon and most of the next day locating a transmission in town and installing it. Without his help, we never would have been able to continue.

More than two days behind schedule now, we set out for our first clinic the following afternoon. For three days, we worked as quickly as we could in stifling hot, unsanitary conditions on four separate plantations serving the poor harvesting community.

As exhausting as those days were, I loved every minute. We learned each new procedure as we went along. We registered patients, conducted simple physical exams, tested urine and blood, and dispensed medicine with the aid of our *PDR* (*Physician's Desk Reference*).

Nanci and I were the only ones besides Ruland who knew any Spanish, so we also became interpreters. We were constantly downing soft drinks to keep up our energy. Meals were cooked by the locals. We'd take a short break, run to one of their homes for a bite of food, and then return to the waiting lines.

Patients walked for miles in the intense heat to bring a sick child or elderly relative to us. They waited hours to be seen. Most suffered from dysentery, typhoid, malaria, or respiratory infections.

We turned a local church into a clinic, using sheets to partition off examining rooms. One wall became the pharmacy where our supplies were spread out and grouped according to the diseases they treated. The opposite wall was lined with benches, where those who had been registered waited for their turn.

The lab was outside. Our one microscope needed direct sunlight to operate, so our parasite expert huddled over it all day, getting a painful sunburn. Nanci shuffled from one examining room to the next, a stethoscope around her neck and patient charts in her hands. I took care of registration.

"What is the problem?" I asked one man in my high school Spanish.

"*Hepatiti,*" he hoarsely breathed back.

"What?" I questioned again.

He put his mouth close to my face. "H-e-p-a-t-i-t-i."

I looked at his eyes, and they were the darkest yellow I'd ever seen. Quickly finishing his questionnaire, I helped him to a spot on the bench.

I registered three more hepatitis victims that morning. Then I opened one of the medical reference books to see if hepatitis is contagious. It is. Quite.

"What's the treatment for hepatitis?" I asked one of the doctors over lunch.

"Plenty of rest and a special diet for most cases. But resting means no income for these people. And they can't afford the cost of a special diet. So they'll probably just keep working until they die."

Our last day of the clinic, we worked a 12-hour shift in order to see every waiting person. As we tore down the makeshift examining rooms, boxed up medication, and organized files, we noticed that a number of people were still there. They were some of the Christians on the plantation who were part of Ruland's congregation. They had waited to help us clean up, and then asked if we could have a worship service before we left.

As tired as we were, we were happy to sing and pray together, and it was an appropriate end to our work, for it reminded me of why we had come—to share Christ's love.

Our group returned to Belize City for a final farewell evening before the Canadians flew home and we returned to the campus. We had made reservations at a recommended hotel, The Bonaventure.

Bonaventure was French for "good adventure."

The women were shown to a large, bare room with eight metal bunk beds on a dusty, cement floor. There were fresh brown pellets on the top bunks.

"What are these?" I asked.

"Rat droppings," the concierge nonchalantly explained. We asked for another room.

We were moved to one which didn't have droppings on the beds, but had holes in the walls large enough for anything to come through at night. We plugged the holes with our pillows before we retired, but could hear the scurrying of little feet in the walls all night long.

Four-inch cockroaches appeared from every crevice in search of food. Nanci tried to kill one—chasing it with a shoe as it flew around the room. The rest of us ducked for cover. My toes stuck through the sheets out of holes that had been gnawed through the material. We slept with the lights on. Actually, I don't think any of us slept. The hotel was aptly named; it was an adventure.

When we finished our work in Belize, we thought we fully understood what it meant to serve God in the face of adversity. But He had a surprise for us....

20

Guardian Angels Working Overtime
(Nanci)

"I had a friend who tried for six weeks to get into El Salvador, but he finally gave up and went back to the United States," argued our taxi driver. "I wouldn't get my hopes up if I were you."

I wasn't optimistic. We were going to the embassy as a lark more than anything else.

"The government has restricted the number of visas issued to Americans," he continued. "For good reason, too. A lot of them go to help the Communist guerrillas."

I never even dreamed of including El Salvador when Stacy and I drew up our itinerary. Vietnam, Cambodia, Burma, and even Lebanon, maybe. Our entry into each was ultimately barred. But an opportunity to visit El Salvador took us both by surprise.

Our initial interest in the country sprang from a brief layover in San Salvador, the capital, *en route* to Belize. Confined to the airport, we were intrigued by the armed soldiers and anti-rebel posters we saw there.

Neither of us thought of it again until we were preparing to leave Belize, and ran into an American who had worked at an orphanage in San Salvador for over a year.

The year had taken its toll: he was thin and drawn, but passionate about what was happening there. In the midst of civil war, a revival was in full bloom. He couldn't say enough about the American pastor he worked with. The pastor and his family had been living in El Salvador since the outbreak of the civil war in 1979, and now oversaw a sizeable ministry.

The reason our new friend had come to Belize, of all places, was for some "rest and recreation." He was exhausted from constantly having to dodge exploding telephone poles, buses, and shops.

We asked if he thought there was any way for us to visit the pastor. A few hours later, we had made all the necessary arrangements. All except one: a visa.

We pulled up in front of the El Salvadoran embassy. "This is your stop, ladies," the driver said. "Lotsa luck."

"I'll need three pictures from each of you," the clerk said. My heart sank. I had ransacked my luggage that morning and had only been able to come up with two.

"Could you just Xerox one of these?" I asked hesitantly as I handed her my pictures. From my previous embassy experiences, I had little hope.

"Sure. Just write down your passport information. I'll fill out the applications for you, and you can pick them up in an hour."

I stared at her in disbelief. "You mean we can go?"

"Yes. Your visas are good for a week."

As our van wound through the isolated countryside, I was sure the jungles on either side of us hid guerrillas. It was almost pitch black by now, and shadows of the swaying trees were ominous. It wasn't unusual for rebels to commandeer vans on this road and leave the passengers stranded overnight. They used the vans to launch attacks on government posts.

I remembered the scene in the movie *Salvador,* in which American nuns were murdered on this very road. The only other time we had faced such acute physical danger was in the Philippines. It was hard to believe that more than a year had passed since then. In less than two weeks, we would be back in the United States.

The other occupants of our van were all Salvadoran. None of them seemed nervous, so I relaxed a little. Still, I felt a sense of relief when we transferred to a city cab for the ride to the church.

Even by night, we could see that the church was a sprawling white building with red trim. Its grounds were immaculately groomed and surrounded by a high black wrought-iron fence. It was quite a contrast from Belize, where all the buildings were either brown or gray depending on how weather-beaten they were. Over the door was a neatly lettered sign: *Voz de Amor* (Voice of Love).

Tiptoeing past three well-armed government soldiers, we made our way into the sanctuary, where the Sunday night service was just ending. An intense man in his early 40s wearing a cowboy shirt was narrating a slide show.

When he finished speaking, we rushed forward to introduce ourselves to the man—Doug Wellborn. Then we joined his teenaged son and daughter waiting in a pickup truck out front.

"You girls must be hungry," he said. "We'll get something to eat on the way to the guest house. It'll give us a chance to talk."

We stopped at a donut shop, and he began to tell us about this city he called home. "Under no circumstances should you ever venture out alone. I'll come and pick you up each day." To illustrate his point, he added, "Two Americans were killed in a shooting incident at another donut shop near here. They were easy targets, because they went to the same place too often. They should have known to vary their routine."

We rode in silence the rest of the way. Stacy and I exchanged worried glances. I wondered: had we come this far just to end up as statistics on some official's tally sheet? We were staying in a large, Spanish-style house with a courtyard which separated the living room and kitchen from a long row of bedrooms. The bedrooms could only be entered from the courtyard. In addition to the occasional missionary passing through, the place housed permanent church workers.

The house and yard were protected by a strong metal fence and a barking German shepherd. "Everyone has dogs here to guard against burglary," Doug said.

We awoke, eager to explore the city. But remembering Doug's words, we decided to wait for him. He arrived an hour late.

"Sorry I'm late, I had to pick up some materials to repair the house. We'll go to the church and I'll tell you about some of our ministries."

The city was much less menacing by daylight. There was little evidence of war. The streets were crowded with people going about their business, seemingly oblivious to the conflict that marred their country.

"The rebels want to destroy the country's economy and blame the government," Doug said. "That way they'll get support for their cause. See that telephone pole over there?" Steel reinforcement rods were all that remained of the four-foot midsection of a concrete telephone pole, and all that kept it from collapsing.

"The rebels try to blow up one pole a day. They want to destroy the communications system. That's why there are so many soldiers around our church. The building across the street is a telecommunications building. Guerrillas attacked it two weeks ago. Churches are big targets. Guerrillas try to seize them as bases to launch assaults."

"Why churches?" I asked.

"Since most government soldiers are devout Catholics, they would never attack a church."

"I came here with my family in 1978, when our youngest was only nine months old, just before the war," Doug said. "When the fighting started, we stayed on as long as we could. Then things got so bad that the organization we were working for forced us to return to the States.

"We desperately wanted to come back. We scraped together all the money we could, and came back with $400 to begin our own ministry.

"The war was much worse in the early years. Just recently, it's started to escalate again, especially in San Salvador. Not a day goes by that there isn't some sort of confrontation."

"But the people don't seem afraid at all," I said.

"They used to be afraid. Now they're just resigned."

"What about you?"

"I refuse to live in fear. God has work for us to do here, and He will protect us."

He paused a moment and rubbed his forehead. "Let me tell you a story. One night, my neighbor was shot in the middle of the night. I heard the noise and ran to help him. I should have waited until I knew it was safe, but it was a good thing I didn't. In the last seven minutes of his life, I led him to the Lord."

———————

I gained an even deeper respect for Doug's ministry one rainy night when we went with him to visit shut-ins.

"When was Doug supposed to pick us up?" I asked Stacy as I pulled on my raincoat.

"About an hour ago, which means he'll be here soon."

Just then Doug dashed in. "I had some errands to run," he apologized.

Stacy and I strode down the wet streets, trying to keep up with Doug's long gait. Going from home to home for prayers and fellowship reminded me of our time with David Stitt in Singapore.

As we hurried down a darkened street, Doug pointed to an empty lot. "One night, my wife and I were caught in cross fire between government and rebel troops over there. We hid underneath our motorcycle until there was a brief pause in the attack. At that moment, a man appeared, seemingly out of thin air, and pointed the way to safety through a tangle of alleyways. We never would have gotten out if he hadn't shown us the way. As soon as we escaped, the fighting started up again. We turned to thank our new friend, but he had disappeared as mysteriously as he had appeared. I think he was an angel."

A loud peal of thunder rang out and I jumped. It sounded like gunfire. Stacy laughed at me until I pointed to her trembling hands.

"See that military outpost? It's been attacked by guerrillas eight times in the past six months," Doug said.

We reached our last home for the night. When we knocked, a man cautiously asked our identity through a crack in the door. He opened it when he recognized Doug's voice, and waved us inside.

"Because I'm a government official, my life is constantly in danger," he said. "The terrorists have an assassination campaign against people with government ties. A few weeks ago, as I was returning from work, guerrillas threw five fire bombs at my car. None of them detonated."

He shook his head, astonished. "They always go off."

Two days later, we waited for Doug to pick us up, glancing at our watches every few minutes. He was running late again. Our bus left for Guatemala in a couple of hours. It was at least a 45-minute ride to the station, and we had things to do on the way.

We had spoken at Doug's church the night before, and he presented us with plaques to remind us to pray for El Salvador. We posed for a picture with the soldiers outside the church; us with our Bibles and them with their guns.

"Sorry I'm late," Doug panted. "I had to drive a woman to the hospital, and now I have to stop by the church."

Passing an empty car in the middle of the street, Doug said, "Sometimes the rebels seize people's cars or even hire taxis to get to an attack site. But because they pride themselves that theirs is a people's revolution, they record the owner's name and address so they can return the car when they're finished with it. A woman from our church has had hers taken three times. She got it back each time."

We arrived at the station just as our bus was pulling out. Doug jumped out of the car and flagged it down. We quickly said our goodbyes and climbed aboard.

That night, in our Guatemalan hotel room, I was awakened from a deep sleep by a frighteningly familiar sound. It was louder and closer than anything we'd experienced in El Salvador. Stacy sat up and looked at me in terror.

"Stacy," I whispered urgently, "hit the deck!"

"I can't move."

"Neither can I."

"Maybe it's not what we think," Stacy reasoned.

"But what if it is? It sounds like they're trying to take over the hotel!"

"I can't remember if there are any camps in this town or not."

She was interrupted by loud staccato sounds. My heart pounded in my throat. We'd made it around the world, and now we were going to die on the last night of our trip. We huddled in the closet for what seemed hours until the noise died away. I crawled over to the window. The sun was coming up, and I could hear people in the hotel stirring.

"I think it's okay to come out now," I said.

We dressed quickly and went downstairs to check out. Our flight to the United States left in a few hours.

"What happened last night? Was there an attack?" Stacy asked the desk clerk, who was drawing up our bill.

"Oh, there was a big religious festival here early this morning before the sun came up. Everyone in town came out to celebrate."

"What was all the noise?"

He laughed. "Fireworks."

21

For the Love of the Harvest (Stacy)

We deliberately made our reentry into the "real" world, as our family and friends called it, as painless as possible. Upon returning to the States, we spent several weeks with our respective families, resting and seeing as few outsiders as possible.

Now we stood on the curb at the Washington airport, where we had begun our journey 16 months earlier. I had often wondered what it would feel like to be back home. One of our friends had offered to house us temporarily, and we were waiting for her to pick us up. I looked up at a plane that had just taken off, and wished I was on a plane again. Going anywhere.

I tired quickly of fielding the same questions and trying to describe 16 life-changing months. Telling my stories was sharing a part of me too private and too precious to trivialize in social conversation. Now we were back in D.C. and could find a way to settle down again. If possible.

On the drive to our friend's home, conversation was sparse and strained. She rattled on about people we had never met, and friends we had known who had left the area.

Finally, she pulled over to the curb and turned to face us. "I think I know how you're feeling. When I returned from mission work in Mexico, I didn't want to be around anyone. And I wasn't gone half as long as you were. You have to give yourselves time."

I couldn't believe the changes since we'd left: an oat bran craze had taken over the food industry, ordinary people walked around with pagers and beeping watches, cellular phones were all over the place. Even our favorite bakery had been replaced by a diet center. The first time I turned on the television, I saw an exhibition of dwarf tossing (the sport of throwing midgets)! The country had fallen apart in our absence.

When I hung up the receiver, Nanci could see that I was upset.

"That was my boss. They've been holding a position open for me, even better than the one I had before, and it pays more money. I have a few weeks to decide." I had been praying about what I should do, but still had no answer. Now other people were asking me, too.

"Well, I don't know about you, but I'm not ready to go back to work," Nanci said. "I don't really know what I want to do. And, of course, we do have that book to write."

We didn't leave the house much that first week back in Washington, but we did look forward to going to our old church on Sunday. We waved as we spotted friends in the congregation. Afterward, we exchanged hugs, new phone numbers, and promises to get together. I was sure someone would invite me to brunch, but everyone had plans.

When the church emptied, I went to find Nanci. She came toward me, shuffling flyers she'd collected from the current events table. Her mood was about as bad as mine.

We went back to the house alone. Nanci made coffee; I made eggs. We waited for the phone to ring.

Our trip to the mailbox became the highlight of each day. We'd peek through the blinds as the postman deposited the mail, wait until he'd left, and then rush out to sort its contents.

It was during this period in our readjustment that God began to answer our prayers in surprising ways.

The first letter arrived from Australia. It was from a young man we'd met in Nepal who wanted to thank us for our help during his "doubting period." He had gone back to reading the Bible and praying daily.

Barb from the Philippines wrote to say how timely our visit had been. She'd been hungry for American companionship, and appreciated the encouragement we'd given her during conversations that ran way into the night. "God sent two angels when I needed them," her letter said.

Mail poured in from Nepal, the Philippines, Indonesia, Singapore, Amsterdam, El Salvador. Daily our spirits were renewed.

But one piece of mail brought me more pain than peace. It was a card from my former co-workers, welcoming me back. Each one expressed how much they looked forward to my return to work. I buried the card in the bottom of a drawer.

We spent days sorting through all the things we'd left in storage, deciding what to keep, give away, or throw away. Most of my old possessions had lost their appeal. One afternoon, I loaded the car and drove to the Goodwill truck a few miles away.

The truck was guarded that day by a thin man with straight black hair and an Asian skin tone. His name tag read Truong.

"Are you from Vietnam?" I asked. "I wanted to go there when I was in Asia, but I couldn't."

He acknowledged that he was indeed Vietnamese.

"When I was in Thailand, I saw some of the refugee camps," I said. I started to name a few until he stopped me.

"That was mine. I remember the missionaries who came to the camp. That's why I'm a Christian."

"God bless you," he called out as I drove away.

Soon, the phone began to ring, and our calendar filled up. By day, we organized files, transcribed tapes, and made notes for our book. By night, we bounced between friends' houses, slide shows, and speaking engagements.

I enjoyed visiting with old friends more than when we had first returned, yet an emptiness was still within me. My world had changed greatly; theirs very little. They talked about weddings, babies, and new cars. I talked about leading Bible studies by kerosene light in Filipino villages or sharing a meal of *chapatis* and lentils with a Pakistani family.

Nanci and I now watched world news in a new way. A coup attempt in the Philippines prompted a discussion about the night we raced through enemy territory in a jeep. We rejoiced when the Nepalese government began releasing Christians from prison. We cried when fighting broke out in San Salvador again.

I continued to wonder which world I fit in. This home wasn't home to me anymore.

We were setting up another slide show. It was our twenty-first, each one different, but this was a very significant one. The guests were the friends who had been at our going-away party.

I was amazed at the different reactions we'd received at each show. At one, for a singles group, people fidgeted and obviously couldn't wait for us to be finished so they could have some refreshments and "mingle." (Yet from that presentation, two people signed up for a summer mission trip.) At the next show, the audience complained that it was too short and begged to hear more. Most receptions fell somewhere in between.

Tonight, the atmosphere was very different from the elaborate party these friends had thrown for us before we left. A wrinkled sheet hung from the ceiling to serve as a screen. Stereo speakers were moved into the room for the musical accompaniment to our slides.

For more than an hour, people sat on the floor or stood

against the walls, watching our show. I completely lost track of time. Nanci and I took turns sharing our experiences.

There were gasps when we told of sleeping with rats, and winces when we listed the things we'd eaten. They were enthralled with our descriptions of riding elephants through Nepalese jungles, and enraged when we described the methods we used to dodge pinches from Muslim men.

After the slides, a friend led us in song: "He is Lord, He is Lord...." The words carried new meaning. I closed my eyes to conceal a tear when I sang, "Every knee shall bow, every tongue confess that Jesus Christ is Lord."

Every knee, every tongue. I could see them.

Then we sang "This is My Father's World." And I knew that to be true.

As I looked into everyone's eyes, I saw that they realized for the first time the magnitude of our journey.

"Do you have any questions?" Nanci asked, finally breaking the silence that had fallen over the room.

"What was your favorite place?"

"Weren't you ever scared?"

"Didn't you get sick or homesick?"

Then from the back of the room came the most important question of all: "Would you do it all again?"

"Oh, yes," I said. "We both would. And we will."

I knew then what answer to give my boss.

Recomended Reading From Youth With A Mission

- **Is That Really You, God?**, by Loren Cunningham ($6.99 US)
  In this book you will see how an ordinary man who was committed to hearing God and obeying Him, became the founder of an extraordinary missionary organization. This book is a practical guide to heaering the voice of God.

- **Daring to Live on the Edge: The Adventure of Faith and Finances,** by Loren Cunningham ($7.99 US)
  A compelling, fresh look at the subject of faith and finances/ trust and provision by one of America's premier missions statesmen. This book will challenge and equip all who want to obey God's call, but who wonder where the money will come from.

- **Stepping Out,** compiled by Hawthorne, Moy & Krekel ($7.99 US)
  This book is a tool to motivate, clarigy expectations, inform of options, shape attitudes and help you adjust to new cultures and working conditions. *Stepping Out* is a powerful resource for those who are preparing for short term mission involvement or work in any capacity related to training and placement for support of missions.

- **Friend Raising,** by Betty Barnett ($8.99 US)
  "*Friend Raising* brings together God's plan for Biblical missions support, with principles proven in the field. The book is a strong dose of common sense, miced with that rare spice, respect for the donor, and liberally garnished with the conviction that God supplies needs through mutually satisfying relationships. In a world overwhelmed by fund raising hype and gimmicks, Betty Barnett presents a refreshing Biblical alternative."

- **Unveiled At Last,** by Bob Sjogren ($7.99 US)
  Have you ever felt that your Christianity was similar to a puzzle? You've got thousands of pieces representing Bible stories, doctrine, the teachings of Jesus, but you're not quite sure where it's all leading to? Bob Sjogren helps you discover a unifying theme woven in the Scripture from Genesis to Revelation, unveiling the very heart of God in a fresh new way.

FREE shipping at book rate when your order any of these books (payment must accompany order).

YWAM Publishing
P.O. Box 55787
Seattle, WA 98155 USA
tel. (206) 771-1153